THE NEW MANAGER'S HANDBOOK

The *Briefcase Books* Series

Managing Stress: Keeping Calm Under Fire
Barbara J. Braham

Business Negotiating Basics
Peter Economy

Straight Answers to People Problems
Fred E. Jandt

Empowering Employees through Delegation
Robert B. Nelson

The Presentation Primer: Getting Your Point Across
Robert B. Nelson
Jennifer Wallick

Listen for Success: A Guide to Effective Listening
Arthur K. Robertson

THE NEW MANAGER'S HANDBOOK

Brad Lee Thompson

IRWIN
Professional Publishing

Burr Ridge, Illinois
New York, New York

© RICHARD D. IRWIN, INC., 1995

Senior sponsoring editor: Cynthia A. Zigmund
Project editor: Beth Yates
Production manager: Laurie Kersch
Designer: Heidi J. Baughman
Art manager: Kim Meriwether
Compositor: Wm. C. Brown Communications, Inc.
Typeface: 10.5/12 Palatino
Printer: Book Press, Inc.

Library of Congress Cataloging-in-Publication Data

Thompson, Brad Lee.
    The new manager's handbook/Brad Lee Thompson.
       p.   cm.—(The Briefcase books series)
    Includes index.
    ISBN 1-55623-925-4 (hardcover).—ISBN 0-7863-0206-2 (softcover)
    1. Management—Handbooks, manuals, etc. 2. Supervision of
employees—Handbooks, manuals, etc. I. Title. II. Series.
HD38.15.T48   1994
658—dc20
                            94–143

Printed in the United States of America

1 2 3 4 5 6 7 8 9 0 BP 1 0 9 8 7 6 5 4

To Susan, David, and Kathleen

The Briefcase Books Series

Research shows that people who buy business books (1) want books that can be read quickly, perhaps on a plane trip, commuting on a train, or overnight, and (2) feel their time and money were well spent if they get two or three useful insights or techniques for improving their professional skills or helping them with a current problem at work.

Briefcase Books were designed to meet these two criteria. They focus on necessary skills and problem areas, and include real-world examples from practicing managers and professionals. Inside these books you'll find useful, practical information and techniques in a straightforward, concise, and easy-to-read format.

This book and others like it in the Briefcase Books series can quickly give you insights and answers regarding your current needs and problems. And they are useful references for future situations and problems.

If you find this book or any other in this series to be of value, please share it with your co-workers. With tens of thousands of new books published each year, any book that can simplify the growing complexities in managing others needs to be circulated as widely as possible.

Robert B. Nelson
Series Editor

Foreword

My mission in life has been to be a conveyor of simple truths. It is for that reason that I'm pleased to be able to introduce the Briefcase Books series, which seeks to provide simple, practical, and direct answers to the most common problems managers face on a daily basis.

It has been my experience that in the field of business common sense is not common practice. So it is refreshing to find a series of books that glorifies common sense in dealing with people in the workplace.

Take the skill of listening. We all know that it is important to listen, yet how many of us actually do it well? I suggest it would be rare to find one in a hundred managers that is truly a good listener. Most people focus on what they are going to say next when someone else is talking. They would seldom if ever think to check what they thought they heard to make sure it is accurate. And they seldom acknowledge or attempt to deal with emotions when they occur in speaking with someone at work. These are basic errors in the use of this basic skill. And regardless of how much education or experience you have, you should know how to listen.

But how much training have you had on the topic of listening? Have you ever had a course on the topic? Have you ever tested your ability to listen? Have you ever discussed with others how you could listen better with greater comprehension and respect? Probably not. Even though this fundamental interpersonal skill could cripple the most talented individual if he or she is not good at it.

Fortunately, listening is just one of the fundamental skills singled out for its own volume in the Briefcase Books series. Others include books on making presentations, negotiating, problem solving, and handling stress. And other volumes are planned even as I write this.

The Briefcase Books series focuses on those basic skills that managers must master to excel at work. Whether you are new to managing or are a seasoned manager, you'll find these books of value in obtaining useful insights and fundamental knowledge you can use for your entire career.

Ken Blanchard
Co-author
The One Minute Manager

Preface

If you just became a manager for the first time, this book is for you.

This book will also help you if you are a new supervisor, a new foreman, a new leader of a work team, or a new group coordinator. Never mind if you don't have "manager" in your job title. Anyone who must accomplish organizational goals through the efforts of others is, in fact, doing the work of a manager. (For our purposes, manager is a gender-neutral term—it describes both men and women. I'll use both "he" and "she" as a reminder that many managers are women.)

Right now, you probably feel a little excited and a little anxious about your new assignment. You also may feel a bit unprepared, which is why this book is going to be helpful.

Chapters 1 through 7 address the basics you need to know as you begin your career as a manager. They explain what is expected of you as a manager and how you can meet—and exceed—those expectations. Here you will find the four-part model of management functions (plan, organize, influence, and control). This model will provide a framework for many of your managerial decisions and actions. It is also a useful way to think about your performance and skill development.

Chapters 8 through 12 give suggestions for building high performance in the workplace. Here are detailed explanations of skills and techniques you can use to build and grow high performance work teams. This section suggests proactive, empowering strategies to use when you have the luxury of time to assess your team members' strengths, weaknesses, and their anticipated needs. These chapters include discussions about performance reviews, delegation, networking, and supervising team members with diverse cultures.

The final chapters of the book provide troubleshooting guidelines for the new manager. It's inevitable that some problems will land on your desk in a sorry mess that you have to clean up. This section features short descriptions of common problems that can be solved by the practical application of your skills, judgment, and common sense. The problems described include problem employees, substance abuse, stealing, insubordination, sexual harassment, absenteeism, conflict resolution, how to say no when you have to, and how to manage your job-related stress. Finally, Chapter 17 closes the book with tips for developing and managing *your* career.

You may already realize that being a manager means continually learning while on the job. However, do not rely solely on trial-and-error experiences to teach you how to be an effective manager. Invest time with this book instead. There are just too many ways to manage poorly, and the sooner you start learning how to manage well, the better!

Like you, I am a hands-on manager. I believe passionately that the new manager makes a critical contribution to the productivity, and therefore the profitability, of his or her organization. Nevertheless, the new manager's ideas, enthusiasm, and talents are too often undervalued, ignored, or wasted simply because he or she is unproven. I want to help you make the most of this opportunity by getting started right.

I hope you find this book useful. I have written this to be a resource that can get you started quickly, establish your credibility with your co-workers, and serve as a foundation for your ongoing training and development needs.

One request: like you, I value feedback. Please give me your comments and suggestions about this book so I can make it even more useful when it is updated. I am especially interested in knowing how you actually use this book. Does it help you in your new role right away? Do you go back to it again and again, or will it just gather dust? What works, what doesn't work, and what can I change or add to make the next edition better? Feel free to give me a piece of your mind! You can write me at 4600 Longfellow Avenue, Minneapolis, MN 55407-3638.

Thanks for the opportunity to help! I wish you much success.

Brad Thompson

Contents

Chapter One

Making the Change from Worker to Manager

Yesterday, you were one of the group. Today, you're the boss. Congratulations on your promotion!

Take a moment to catch your breath and give yourself some credit. You must be doing a lot of good work. Your managers obviously believe they are doing the right thing for the company by putting you in charge.

If you *don't* have time to catch your breath, however, it's probably because you have to be on the job tomorrow morning as a new manager. If so, go directly to Chapter 2: *Get Started Right*. As important as this chapter is—it describes the changes you face and why managers succeed and fail—it is not as important as being prepared for day one in your new role as a manager!

This book will help you if you are a new supervisor, a new foreman, a new leader of a work team, or a new group coordinator. Never mind if you don't have "manager" in your job title. Anyone who must accomplish organizational goals through the efforts of others is, in fact, doing the work of a manager. (For our purposes, "manager" is a gender-neutral term—it describes both men and women. When both "he" and "she" are used, it's a reminder that many managers are women.)

Now you have some choices to make: What kind of boss are you going to be? How are you going to change your relationships with the people you used to work with as peers? Also, you've probably declared more than once that there are better ways to run the company; now that you're in charge, which of your ideas are you going to act on first?

WHAT AM I GETTING MYSELF INTO?

What's that? You say you're not sure you want to be a manager?

Your anxiety is understandable. Until now, your view of management has probably been somewhat one-sided. Maybe you've even had first-hand experience with managers who were difficult to work for because they:

- Gave lots of orders, but rarely listened to new ideas.
- Said little about what was going on elsewhere in the company.
- Failed to plan well, which meant you had to work weekends.
- Provided only confusing feedback about your performance.
- Set work team members against each other with favoritism and gossip.
- Generally did not support your efforts to do your job.

Do you recognize anyone you know? Your list could probably go on and on. It is a fact of life that some managers are more effective than others. If you have suffered with a poor manager, you already know a lot about what *not* to do. It's no wonder you are a little anxious: No one wants to be a poor manager, ineffective and causing unhappiness among those who work for him or her.

But it doesn't have to be so. Being a manager can be an immensely satisfying experience for you and those who work for you. By managing the efforts of others, you have more opportunities to make your ideas come to life. You can be a leader, a mentor, a person of vision and action who is respected and rewarded for your contributions to the bottom line and the quality of work life in the company.

Being a manager doesn't suit everyone, but successful new managers give the following reasons why it was worthwhile for them to give up their comfortable, familiar jobs to become managers.

1. *Managers can grow, personally and professionally.* Change can be uncertain and, at times, even uncomfortable, but otherwise sane and healthy people like you are attracted to the ranks of management because they believe they are ready to learn something new, practice new skills, and solve bigger problems.

2. *Managers can make more of a difference.* Being a manager means having a voice that is listened to by those above and below you in the organization. Generally, the higher a person moves in the organization, the more he or she can affect the success of the organization.

3. *Managers get more rewards.* Greater rewards come with greater contributions to the success of the organization. Some rewards are financial; some are preferential, such as a reserved parking space; and some are psychological, such as satisfaction from meeting a new challenge successfully.

What does it really mean to be a manager? Your experience will be unique, of course. The job will probably be more tedious than you expect, harder than you imagined, and almost certainly lacking the dreamed-of glamour and power. You will have to get used to the idea that you are getting paid to have difficult conversations with people, and you will be amazed that you have to talk to them about everything from their poor performance to their offensive hygiene!

You will be disappointed to find that you cannot change the organization overnight. You may become discouraged when you have to live with contradictions, paradoxes, and unresolved situations. And you may find yourself perpetually frustrated with office politics, pointless meetings, bureaucratic pettiness, indecision from above and below, shifting priorities, and chronic lack of time and resources.

You may even discover that you were promoted for the wrong reasons. It may not matter as much as you think that you have been successful so far because you work hard, contribute consistently, and demonstrate a commitment to the organization and its values. The fact that you are a good worker, a seasoned employee who knows the routines, or a nice person may have little bearing on your future success as a manager. Superior sales people do not always make good sales managers, and an excellent staff worker may be only a mediocre staff leader. Managing requires you to learn new skills, adopt a broader perspective, and make deeper commitments.

So can *you* be a successful manager? Maybe. You have quite a bit going for you already because you have the confidence of your managers; in their opinion, you have the right combinations of intelligence, interpersonal skills, work habits, and company knowledge to be successful. Your work so far has met their expectations.

You also have your recent experience working in your favor. Because you know firsthand the problems and conditions out on the assembly line or back in the claims department, you are in an excellent position to remedy the problems.

In addition, you have this book. The no-nonsense coaching found herein will help you to anticipate the challenges you will face, solve specific problems along the way, and, most of all, keep things in perspective.

I LIKE AND RESPECT MY FRIENDS. NOW THAT I'M THEIR BOSS, WHAT SHOULD I EXPECT?

Expect the best, but be prepared for some lingering resentment and occasional tests of your authority. Nancy Adams, a new marketing manager, heard the following comments from her former peers within the first few days after her promotion; notice how Nancy responded:

Friend 1
Congratulations Nancy—you're going to be great!

Nancy

Thank you! I think we're all going to be a great team!

Friend 2

I'm glad they finally put someone in charge who knows what it's like out in the field. Can we get new dealer sales kits now?

Nancy

I don't know yet, but I know it's important to you, so it's going to be one of the first concerns I address. I'll let you know by next week.

Friend 3

I don't like the new compensation plan, Nancy. And you wouldn't like it either if you weren't a supervisor now.

Nancy

Do you think I'm suddenly somehow a different person now? I have never automatically agreed with you or anyone else in the past. Remember the new cooperative advertising program? I told you then I thought you were wrong. I'm an individual, and I bring my own ideas, values, and experiences to the job.

Friend 4

Sure, I resent you—you're younger than I am, and I have more experience. I always thought of you as a friend, but I can see now that you're just like everybody else, just looking out for yourself.

Nancy

I'm sorry you feel that way. You know I've earned this promotion. When you are less upset, I hope we can talk about this differently. I still regard you as a valuable member of the team, and we'll still need your help to achieve our goals. Think this over, and let's talk tomorrow.

People who were once your co-workers may have feelings of resentment or envy toward you because of your promotion. They will also have concerns, such as what your new position will mean for them and their careers.

You may lose some friends. If you used to work with the people you are now supervising, you can expect some awkward moments. Some people may no longer wish to see you socially. Others may try to take advantage of your new position; if they perceive you as their friend at the top, you may be expected to look the other way when rules are bent, grant special favors, and generally make their lives easier. Whether you are supervising a group of people with whom you are very familiar or not familiar at all, you can expect to be tested. In either case, prepare to prove yourself after a short honeymoon period.

At the end of the day, you may have to earn back your friends' trust and respect. "I didn't lose my friends when I became their manager," recalls one department chief, "but I had to redefine my relationship with them. We had to learn new ways of talking about work, because now I knew how much money they made and how many mistakes they were responsible for. Sometimes it was awkward, but we just kept talking. It took a couple of months. We had to reassure each other and demonstrate all over again that we could trust each other to be fair and honest. After that, things were better than ever on our team because we built on the strength of our prior relationships."

With time, your old and new friends will see what kind of manager you are. Be yourself, and make an extra effort to communicate your values and commitments. People will eventually understand that you are more than just your last job, your current job, or your next job.

NOW THAT I AM A MANAGER, WHAT ELSE IS DIFFERENT?

Now your job is to get the expected results from your work group. Before you became a supervisor, your responsibility was limited to the tasks you personally performed. You probably did not have to lose sleep when someone in your department did not do their job—unless, of course, you were the one assigned to work overtime to make it right!

Now your chief responsibility is to see that all the work of your department gets done and gets done properly. *You* must plan and organize the resources to accomplish the objectives of your work group, and *you* must hold yourself accountable for your work group's results. Now it is your job to help everyone else complete their work successfully, and to assign the overtime if they don't! You do this by:

- Learning much more about your company's goals and understanding how your department contributes to those goals.
- Setting and communicating the priorities that guide your work team's day-to-day activities.
- Developing and implementing good work plans that get the work finished on time and within budget.
- Providing direction and feedback to your co-workers about their job performance.

Now you see the "big picture."   You now look at the company with a wider view, a broader perspective. The Latin root of the word *supervision* means "to see over, to see from above." This is the management point of view you share with other managers.

Rather than focusing on one isolated bit of work activity, you are concerned with big picture questions: What work is in progress? What do we have to do to get ready for it? Who is doing what, and will they finish on time? What resources can we commit to solving the quality problems that came up in the employee meeting? Is the department within its budget? Can we improve productivity by buying new equipment, or would we save more time by changing the way we process finished parts?

Looking at the big picture does not free you from details. On the contrary, details about production, material costs, scheduling, budgets, and many other subroutines are important pieces of the management puzzle. Sometimes working with the smallest details provides the clues with which you can solve the big problems. But details can be seductive time traps. They can create the illusion of making progress simply because they make you feel busy. For example, to spend three days evaluating software may be a necessary exercise for you, or it may be a waste of your time because it is a task that could and should be delegated.

Time really is money, and your time just became more valuable to the company. You must learn to think critically about problems and opportunities in ways that make the best use of the company's time and money. You must learn to make wise choice about where you direct your efforts. Almost always, your time is better spent thinking about options—the big picture—while your people think about details.

Now you must work through others. Your ideas and plans will never be realized unless and until you have the support of your work team. In turn, you must support their efforts by being the best manager you can be. This almost always means you must spend more time delegating, directing, and coaching and less time doing. You simply cannot assume the time-consuming tasks of managing without giving up the work you used to do.

This is hard. If you used to earn your pay as a millwright or a computer programmer, for example, you are likely to be frustrated with less capable people reporting to you in those positions. You will be tempted to involve yourself in their work because you know it so well. Wouldn't it take less time just to roll up your sleeves, wade into the problems, and fix everything yourself?

Sure, it would be faster—today. But it would be better for the overall success of the company tomorrow if your work team learned to do their jobs without depending on you to save the day. Your challenge is to cause them to depend on you less and depend on themselves more. This is called *empowerment*. Sure, they will let you do their jobs and even let you feel like a hero (why wouldn't they—isn't it easier to stay out of your way?), but what does that really gain for you and the company in the long run? Wouldn't it be better if you coached your workers in ways that enabled them to do their jobs more effectively, perhaps even increasing their skills? This is called *building capacity and capability.*

You help your people learn their jobs better by stepping back and letting them make their own decisions, even if they sometimes make mistakes that cost the company money. This is the best on-the-job training they can get. Now, you are their coach—you must train them and then empower them to learn for themselves by letting them make their own decisions and accept real responsibility.

Don't become a manager who doesn't have time to manage because he's doing everyone else's job. Besides, who knows? Maybe the millwrights or computer programmers reporting to you will come up with some new solutions to old problems. Your experience and know-how is most valuable to the company when you supervise, not when you do the work. Try getting out of the way so your workers can do their jobs, and then go and do yours!

Now you get and give more information. You communicate with more people, more often. You cannot be isolated or insulated. It's your job to know what is going on and to tell your people what is going on so that everyone can work together smoothly.

In most organizations, information is the currency of power. The more you know, the more power you are perceived to have. Corporate mythology says that to share information is to give up power. Actually, the reverse is true: When you share information with your group, you empower them to contribute more to your department's objectives. Then, when the department succeeds, everyone succeeds.

One of your more difficult tasks is to build and manage your information channels. While you are still new to the job is an opportune time to ask your workers all kinds of questions, such as the following:

- What is your job here? Do you like your job? What do you especially like or dislike about your job? How do you know when you are doing your job well?
- What does this department do?
- How does this department get evaluated?
- Who are the customers of this department, both inside and outside the company, and what are they saying about us?

Later on, after you have some experience with your new responsibilities, you can ask:

- How are we doing?
- What obstacles are keeping us from serving our customers—both internal and external—in the ways they want us to?
- Do we share a common, accurate understanding of what is really going on around here?
- Do we share a common vision of who we are?
- Do we agree on what our priorities are?
- What are our plans for the next three days? The next three weeks? The next three months?

Some people will give you too much information because they want to impress you with their accomplishments or campaign for their favorite projects. Other people will be reluctant to share what they know because they are not willing to accept the responsibility that goes along with being an empowered worker (these folks prefer to keep a low profile, volunteer for nothing, and do only what they are told).

Further complicating your communication will be the blizzard of memos, correspondence, and trade journals landing on your desk. What's really important? What information needs to be passed on to others? What other information are you not receiving and need to go out and get? Is everyone learning what they need to know? Are you getting an accurate understanding of what's going on around you?

How can you be sure your information channels are uncluttered, quick, and reliable? A quick way to check is to ask yourself one question: Is anyone getting surprised? Few surprises in business are pleasant. Surprises are symptoms of unclear or incomplete communication. If you, your workers, or your boss receive one too many nasty surprises, exercise your managerial authority to get more of the right information.

Now you solve problems. Better yet, you anticipate potential problems and dismantle them before they cost time and money to fix. Among managers, this is called "getting in front of the snowball" in order to stop it before it rolls down-hill, out of control, getting bigger all the time. You are no longer a bystander; now you are paid to solve and prevent problems.

Now you work with other managers.   You have a new set of peers now: other managers. Together, you comprise the leadership of the company. You need to support each other in a variety of ways.

Mark Gordon stumbled into an awkward situation with another member of the management team after he had been a supervisor for about two months. Here's what he was hearing from his workers: "Mark, the supervisor of the other department is not as strict as you are. They do not have to make up time when they come in late or leave early or take a long lunch hour. You're nit-picking about a few minutes here and there."

Mark was stumped for a good response: "I don't know what to say. I'm following company policy. All I can say is that I'll talk to Marie in the other department."

"Good. We want to do it their way. As it is, we think the situation is unfair."

Later, Mark was very direct with Marie. "Your relaxed policy about checking in and out is causing me fits," he said. "I'm on the verge of a mutiny over there, and the productivity of my people is on the slide. Why aren't you enforcing the company policy?"

Marie smiled. "Mark, I believe that getting the job done is more important than just rigidly enforcing a policy, Yes, I admit I'm bending the rules. But here's why: most of my workers are seasoned employees who know their jobs better than I ever will. I've relaxed this rule as a way to acknowledge their experience and show the company's trust and respect. They know they have earned my trust; I trust them to always get their jobs done. They also know that the consequence for poor performance will be a stricter check-in and check-out policy."

"But can't you tell them compliance with this policy is part of their job description? Can't you just tell them to do it or find another job?" Mark asked.

"That would be a bit extreme, wouldn't it?" Marie countered. "Do you know how important these people are to our success as a company? You can't easily replace trained people like these. No, I'm not going to change my approach on this. It's taken a long time to get to this point. In my judgment, these people deserve to be treated like adults who do their jobs well. I won't allow any excesses or abuses of my relaxed policy, but I'm not going to become a clock-watcher, either."

Mark found Marie's logic compelling. Her department did have excellent performance and good morale. But what could he do now? He worried that his workers were less experienced and considerably younger.

He decided that he would share Marie's approach with his workers. Perhaps if they understood the responsibilities assumed by Marie's department, a relaxed policy could work for their department, too. At the very least, he would demonstrate that he was sincerely trying to be fair.

Mark learned two lessons from this experience. First, his success depends on the cooperation and aid of other managers as much as his workers. Second, the best policies are the policies that get the job done.

Finally, you are now one of many partners in the success of the business. You are all resources for each other in the enterprise. You are in partnership with your new boss and other senior managers. You are in partnership with your peers, workers, and even your vendors. In a real sense, your new job is to collaborate with your partners so you can all work together for the success of the business.

WHAT MAKES A MANAGER SUCCESSFUL?

Now that you have some understanding of what a manager is and what a manager does, let's explore why some managers succeed and others fail.

A manager is considered successful when performance or results meet or exceed expectations. If you ask a dozen successful managers the reasons for their success, you'll get different answers that sound something like this:

> "I am successful because I routinely asked and answered the manager's three most important questions:
>   What's really going on here?
>   What is the most important task for me to be doing now?
>   And what can I finish today?"

> "When your work group succeeds, you succeed, so you do whatever it takes to help your people succeed."

> "There's dumb luck and smart luck. First, you have to be in—or get to—the right place at the right time. Then, you work like hell to make the most of the opportunity."

> "Teamwork."

> "Planning."

> "Making more right decisions than wrong decisions. And never, never make three big mistakes in a row."

> "Leadership."

> "Learning the difference between the nice-to-do work and the need-to-do work. Do the important stuff first."

> "Reserve your passion for results. Do not become so heavily invested in an idea or approach that you cannot see when it should be dropped."

> "When you're wrong, admit it and move on."

Actually, all of these and more contribute to a manager's success. But no one approach or set of skills will solve every problem.

Learning to manage really means learning to exercise sound judgment and make good decisions. Successful management is a series of decisions that lead to the accomplishment of the organization's objectives. It's not as simple as sorting the right decisions from the wrong decisions, because your options are rarely simply right or simply wrong.

Management requires you to use your best judgment and common sense to choose the trade-offs that will best support the organization when all the options are considered. Was it better in our earlier example for new manager Mark Gordon to relax the rules, enforce the company's policy, change Marie's approach, or ignore the problem altogether? Mark's choices affected the partners who worked for him and worked with him. Like Mark, you have to appreciate the fact that your decisions affect everyone who works with you. From now on, your choices will influence their success.

We can control, or at least affect, our successes and failures through the decisions we make. You understand this already as it relates to your personal life; you must have done enough things right to earn your promotion!

Consider what failure can teach us about success. Failures terrify us as much as successes thrill us. Like our successes, our failures look and feel different to each of us: Getting fired. Being passed over for promotion. Wasting an opportunity. Blowing the budget. Losing a valuable employee. Being reassigned to a dead-end job.

How do you deal with personal failures? Do you try to cover them up, deny they happened, pretend they aren't important? You know you can't anymore. As a manager, you are too visible to get away with that kind of self-deception.

You must understand that most of your failures are of your own making. You cannot learn from mistakes until you acknowledge them for what they are. New managers are especially vulnerable to the myth that they are not allowed to fail. Is this realistic? Which of your senior managers has never failed, suffered a setback, or made a mistake?

You naturally want to prove yourself to reinforce the decision to promote you, but you don't have the luxury of self-deception any longer. Your peers and partners on the management team need your view of reality, not your wish list. If you admit your mistakes and learn from them, your judgment will continue to improve. Next time, better decisions are likely to yield better performance.

Do you see how failures are linked to choices? Quality of decision making always shows up in performance. Did we—our work group or our organization—do our job? Poor judgment leads to poor performance, and poor performance leads to negative consequences. Better judgment means better results, more successes, and fewer failures.

The steps of the corporate ladder can become too slippery for nearly everyone. You can expect to have your share of trips and slips if you continue to climb it.

A recent survey[1] of 191 male and female managers in large companies who considered themselves successful revealed that virtually all had suffered hardship experiences, including missed promotions, firings, and business failures. Each of these managers bounced back from failure. To them, failure was part of the growth process. Failure was the logical outcome of one or more bad decisions; it did not mean they were bad people. The Center for Creative Leadership, a research firm in Greensboro, North Carolina, discovered that these successful managers shared a willingness to accept responsibility for causing their own failure. Rather than blame others, they admitted their mistakes and moved on, sometimes to new jobs, new employers, or new careers. Following are five of the most common causes of self-induced failure identified by the managers.

They are unable to get along. Poor interpersonal skills cause most managers most of their problems. They don't listen enough, they don't share enough information, and they fail to treat subordinates with respect.

"We're glad she's gone," said the program leader at a large computer firm, referring to a former colleague who had just taken a position with another company. "She made happy-talk with us, then asked us—or told us—to help her do her job. She doesn't have a family, but we do. The marathon phone calls at home, the routine weekend work—she drove the staff crazy. She was proud of the fact that she received new assignments every year or so; frankly, I think that's about the time it took to burn out her staffs. Maybe senior management appreciated her ability to get things done, but I don't think they saw the walking wounded she left behind."

Arrogance, disrespect, and other unpleasant attitudes lead to predictable results: alienation, lack of trust, high turnover, and poor morale. And the problems are not limited to subordinates, either—some managers continue to have problems with their peers and bosses, too.

---

[1]E. H. Lindsey, V. Homes, and M. W. McCall, Jr., *Key Events in Executives' Lives* (Greensboro, NC: Center for Creative Leadership, 1987).

They fail to adapt. Sometimes the ideal fit between a talented individual and an organization is stretched to the breaking point when the business, the person, the industry, or the market changes.

"I helped start this division," the unemployed manager complained bitterly. "They needed someone like me who could do the openfield running, make decisions on the fly, think fast, and respond on a moment's notice—oh, what's the use? They've all gone corporate now. I predict they'll blow it within the year."

What was valued in a manager at one time—new ideas or forthright discussion, for example—may not be appreciated forever. A manager's style, priorities, focus of energy, and industry knowledge have to stay up-to-date and continue to match the organization.

They are trapped in the "me only" syndrome. Managers preoccupied with how much recognition they are getting eventually find themselves alone, even though they may make significant contributions on their way up the corporate ladder.

"It was tough toward the end," explains a former manager. "I actually got to the point where I was doing things because they were good for me, not because they were good for the company. Our agendas used to be the same, but somewhere along the way I began behaving as if the company was there to serve my needs, not the other way around. If I were them, I would have fired me, too."

"Me only" managers have trouble leading others and setting their own needs aside for the company's needs. They are hard to work for because they are not authentic team players.

They are afraid to act. One way to avoid failure, some managers reason, is to avoid making risky decisions and delay taking risky actions. In other words, to make yourself a smaller target for criticism by keeping a very low profile. These managers may actually be hard workers who otherwise contribute good ideas but lack the commitment or the courage to move their ideas and plans forward. "Paralysis because of analysis" or "playing it too safe" summarizes their problem. Their inability to come to closure actually puts them at greater risk.

A true story: "A since-departed manager actually took more than a year to study our performance appraisal system and make revisions. He looked busy all that time, but by the time he finished, the department had a whole new staff, including a new manager, and they were happily using a totally different system!"

They are unable to rebound. The Center for Creative Leadership's study found that a manager's ability to recover after a setback was crucial to his or her ultimate success.

Heard at the health club:

"I'd still be on my way up if those imports hadn't ruined the market!"

"It was office politics, plain and simple. You wouldn't believe what the Dragon Lady did to me!"

"Sure, I've had a setback or two, but who hasn't? This thing was a fluke. I'm just going to get back on that horse and ride it again. See, I'm persistent, maybe even a bit stubborn. And I'll keep doing it until my ship comes in; you can bank on that."

Managers who seem to be dogged by failure actually cause more problems for themselves because they react to failure by becoming defensive, trying to conceal it, or blaming others for their misfortunes. These managers have narrow, brittle definitions of success for themselves that require excessive rationalization as protection from the real world.

Successful managers, on the other hand, are resilient. They admit their mistakes, learn their lessons, and strive to do better next time. Since most careers tend to zigzag upward, "the ability to handle failures well can make or break a climb to the top," according to the study by the Center for Creative Leadership.

So, what *does* make a manager successful? It sounds so easy: The successful manager sees to it that the right work gets done in the right way at the right time. To do this, he or she incorporates the corporate priorities and values into a rational decision-making process called good judgment. The successful manager accepts accountability for the good, bad, or mediocre accomplishments of his or her work group. It is never easy and not always fair, but no one ever guaranteed it would be, did they?

CAN I BE A SUCCESSFUL MANAGER?

Sure. It's not brain surgery. And you have this book to help you get started. The basics we'll cover here will provide the foundation for your future development—not a moment invested in yourself with this book will be wasted time. It gets you off on the right foot, fast, and then keeps you moving forward, one problem at a time, in roughly the sequence you'll encounter them.

In the following chapters, we'll describe in detail what a manager does, why it's important, and how to do it well. We'll also examine the nature of your relationships with your workers and develop guidelines for keeping them productive and healthy. We'll look at the good and bad sides of power, communication that works, and the management and measurement of performance. Finally, we'll troubleshoot people problems you're likely to encounter and your challenge to continue your development.

Do you still want to be a manager? It's your choice. Only you can decide if this assignment rewards you well enough to continue. Sometimes you'll love your new job; other times you'll wish you were back on the line with your buddies where life was a lot simpler.

The reluctant manager is a poor manager, so if you choose to proceed, decide to do the best you can do. The world does not need another half-hearted, mediocre manager!

Chapter Two

Get Started Right

Imagine that you are starting your new position as manager tomorrow morning. You are going to dress a bit more carefully, arrive at work a little earlier, and sit in the legendary hot seat of responsibility for the first time.

Let's also imagine that you feel somewhat unprepared for this assignment, but you were coaxed into accepting it by your new boss. Perhaps you were selected because you were the next, best-qualified candidate on the "promotables" list. Perhaps not; maybe your boss simply needed a person, any person, to fill this slot in a hurry. In any case, you are on the receiving end of a less-than-perfect decision in a less-than-perfect world; in other words, your promotion is a typical management decision on the part of your new boss as she tries to make the best use of available resources.

So you have some understandable doubts about how well this promotion is going to work out for you. Still, wouldn't it be satisfying to surprise all those naysayers, skeptics, and scoffers who are betting against you? Wouldn't it be terrific if you made much more of this opportunity than anyone expects?

For a while, you are going to get your chance, so let's make the most of it!

GET STARTED RIGHT, RIGHT NOW

Your immediate challenge is to establish your credibility, and the best way to do that is to demonstrate that you are the best person for your job. Why is personal credibility so important?

Because the weight of your title is not so great that you can simply command someone to get done what needs to get done. You need to work with everyone above, below, and beside you on the corporate ladder. If you are perceived as a person of little credibility, you will not be taken seriously, which means you will not be able to have the types of discussions that yield improved performance, either theirs or yours.

Personal credibility is easy to lose and hard to get back. It is determined by others and built on those values you learned as a child: Say what you mean, mean what you say. Follow through and follow up. Don't let your teammates down. Be someone your team can trust. Be yourself.

For now, don't worry too much about establishing your management style, which is a convenient way of describing how you interact with people. Your unique style will evolve as you get comfortable with your new role. Concentrate instead on the substance of your job. What you choose to get done will speak volumes to those with whom you must establish your credibility. Selecting the right work to do, and finishing it on time and on budget, will show people that you are indeed competent to handle your new job.

Deciding to play it safe by doing nothing, keeping a low profile, staying out of people's way, and generally avoiding conflict is almost always the wrong decision. You are more than a placeholder. You are not doing your job if you do not take a few risks. Be smart, not just safe. In the long run, your best job security will rest on your reputation for getting results.

What's the quickest way to earn such a reputation? Why, to get results, of course! This is where you have to do some careful thinking and develop a bit of a strategy for yourself. You cannot afford to fail at your first few managerial tasks, so choose them wisely.

Enthusiastic new managers are commonly trapped in the "I can do anything for everyone" mindset when they first begin, so they say yes to too many people too soon. Your first few days as a manager will be filled with meetings, introductions, and other hazardous distractions. As the new kid, you are an easy target for everyone who wants to breathe new life into their old ideas ("I need a bright person like you to help me make my lead zeppelin fly"), get someone else (like you) to help them with their agenda, or otherwise prop up their career at your expense. Most of these other people know, but have chosen to forget, that you already have more than enough to keep you busy just learning how to do your new job. Soon, you'll have a sense of which of these people really merit your help and friendship; chances are, the people who would knowingly load you up to fail will not be among your first choices for mentors.

It's true—not everyone is rooting for you. Everyone else has his or her own career to promote, and their agendas do not always include helping out the new guy. You will meet rising stars, falling stars, and dead stars, whiners and winners, and many new breeds of corporate animals, most of whom are more political than you. Don't be in such a big hurry to make new friends that you choose poorly. Your selection of a poor network of friends suggests you are a poor judge of human nature, and this will be noticed by people who really matter.

After a few days of saying yes to all the wrong people, the new manager will be overcommitted. He or she has simply made too many promises to too many people. The only way out of this dilemma is to work 32 hours a day to catch up, go back to all of these people and explain why he or she is going to disappoint them, or pretend that nothing is wrong until the subordinates start complaining. A chronically overcommitted manager cannot be successful. Most of the managerial work you're doing is new, so it will logically take longer to get it done in the beginning.

Instead of rushing into risky commitments indiscriminately, pick a few near-term challenges at which you know you can quickly succeed. If these challenges have a high profile and get you rave reviews from others, so much the better. But don't jeopardize your relationship with your work team for any reason. These people are pivotal to your success. You have to take care of them first, second, and last. You must establish your credibility with your work team with a few early successes, however modest.

One manager earned the respect of his workers quickly by solving something as simple as a weekly scheduling problem. This problem was a constant irritant to the lowest-level workers in the plant because it affected them every day, but it was trivial to everyone else. When he was a plant worker himself, the manager had recognized the problem and suggested a solution that was dismissed; once he became the manager, he moved swiftly to fully understand the latest variation of the problem, seek his workers' involvement, decide, and act. It was simple, important, and quickly done.

Establish your credibility quickly by demonstrating success. What you choose to do first and how well you perform will be watched carefully by those around you, and, fairly or unfairly, they will begin to draw conclusions about you as a manager.

We'll take a big picture look at your role as a manager later in the chapter. Right now, it is more important to discuss what should happen tomorrow and in the coming weeks. You'll only have one chance to make a first impression as a new manager, so think carefully about what you want and need to accomplish; then, begin making several lists like those that follow.

What will you do the first day on your new job? What will you accomplish during the first week? The first month? Following is a list of almost-serious suggestions about what you should be doing to make those first impressions the right impressions and those first steps the right steps. Even though you will probably stumble once or twice in the coming weeks and months, you will at least fall in the right direction!

Day 1

All of the following may need to be done today. Which will I choose to do, and in which order?

I will . . .

- Introduce myself to everyone in my work group.
- Refurnish my office with Italian sculpture.

- Familiarize myself with the records, schedules, budgets, and plans of the person who sat in this chair up until last week; if I can't read them all today, I'll at least know where to find them.

- Take a slow tour of the office and/or plant to familiarize myself with "the feel of the place" and present myself to the work group as a "real" person.

- Start a list of problems I observe (This will usually include inefficiencies that you think you see or know about; do not take action on these problems yet—don't even mention them to anyone—because you haven't the time or wherewithal to verify these as problems yet.).

- Start a list of opportunities I observe (including ideas for saving and making money; I'll keep this list to myself, too).

- Figure out how the phone works; introduce myself to the person who can help me master it in the coming weeks.

- Learn how to turn the computer on and off; also learn who knows how to make the system do what it is supposed to: Improve productivity by saving looking-up time, putting-away time, cross-referencing time, writing time, and number-crunching time.

- Sit in on one of my subordinates' meetings; listen!

- Move into my "space" and make it mine with at least one personal object that will get conversations started (such as a photo of my hunting dogs or my favorite vacation island).

- Resolve not to make promises I cannot absolutely, positively keep, no matter how tempting it is.

- Resolve not to make changes in anything for at least a few weeks, which will give me enough time to consult with the "stakeholders"—those people with interests in what I may change.

- Begin reading everything I can get my hands on, looking for meaningful information about our products and services, customers, and people.

Week 1

All of the following may need to be done this week. Which will I choose to do, and in which order?

I will . . .

- Begin learning immediately what my department does, how it does it, how much it costs to do it, and how good it is; I know that in the not-too-distant-future, I will be asked to make scheduling commitments, product production estimates, manpower calculations, and much more. I want and need to become the resident expert on my department, so learning about this job and this department is my number one priority.

- Begin making requests of others inside and outside the department for information; if I don't get the information promised to me, I ask again.

- Meet casually with each employee for light conversation to learn their name and title, what they do, and a little about them as individuals. I'll go to them on company time so I won't ask them to give up their break time to come and talk to me.

- Meet with each employee again to ask open-ended questions like the following:

    What parts of your job do you really enjoy? (Don't ask for the negative aspects yet, but don't be surprised if they tell you anyway.)

    What suggestions do you have to improve things around here?

    How do you interact with the other people in this work unit? (I will strive to approach people in a nonthreatening, constructive manner so they will feel comfortable sharing their thoughts with me. If I make them feel defensive, I'll get worse than nothing—namely, excuses and bad attitudes; I will also remain noncommittal because I am not sure what really needs to be changed yet, if anything.)

- Meet with my counterparts in other divisions to share experiences, anecdotes, and useful tips; these people will become part of my new network.

- Meet with the corporate furnishings department about repainting the sign on my reserved parking place.

- Select three moderately important and difficult problems to solve this week; then, line them up in order of their importance to the company's goals and solve them completely, one at a time (this will give me first-hand experience with how things really work in my department).

- Meet with my boss several times to discuss his short- and long-term priorities; find out what he thinks is important for me to be working on, how he defines a "success" in my job, and what outputs he values so I can be sure to meet his needs and expectations. In this way, I will have a fighting chance to "manage my manager."

- Continue plowing through the production reports and personnel reports found in the files since I've decided that I must get somewhat familiar with these figures quickly, even if I don't fully understand the significance of what I'm looking at yet. I certainly don't want to get bogged down with analyses yet—that would be like trying to drive the company car forward by only looking in the rear-view mirror. By the way, I'm not asking subordinates to filter the information because I want to "get my hands dirty" first and ask questions later, after I understand it better.

Month 1

All of the following may need to be done this month. Which will I choose to do, and in which order?

I will . . .

- Embark on a mission of cleanliness to tidy all the bulletin boards in the department.

- Continue follow-up meetings with employees who have something to say about some aspect of our problems; I remain the "sympathetic information gatherer" and resist the temptation to fix things just because someone asked me to, so I think I'm building a reputation for being a good listener and for thinking before acting.

- Continue to add to my lists of problems and lists of opportunities (see Day 1 listing).

- Continue to select problems and opportunities requiring action and tackling them completely so they are finished in one way or another; I fear getting lots of things started and getting nothing done; I think I'm getting a nice reputation for being a "finisher," so people seem to be gaining confidence in me.

- Finish my reading of random and general information; now I know what information is most relevant and have assigned myself a short reading list that will keep me abreast of industry, company, and department news and performance.

- Resist the temptation to get drawn into the traps that will take too much of my time; there's still so much to learn, and I can't slow down now!

THE NEW MANAGER MEETS
THE NEW REALITIES

Mark Gordon's second week on the job is going poorly. He is talking with Janice, a staff person from the human resources department.

"What do you mean I have to rehire Jeff?" Mark asks. "I caught him using illegal drugs in the restroom. I fired him for breaking the law, and if I can't do that, you better tell me what I can do, because I'm very confused."

Janice wants to help Mark. She understands his frustration. She does not want to dampen his energy and enthusiasm for his new supervisory job, but he has overstepped his limits this time.

"Mark," she said, "You can't just fire a person. It may be simple from your point of view, but there's a right way and a wrong way."

"You mean there is a slow way and a no way, don't you? He's been pulling this stuff for a long time. Remember, I know that crew like they're my family. I know Jeff is a threat to himself and everyone else back there."

"I appreciate how you feel, but you—meaning the company—can't make this stick. If he has a problem . . ."

"I can't believe what I'm hearing! *If* he has a problem?" Mark exclaimed. "Janice, the guy sells drugs out of his car. His drug store opens every afternoon at quitting time! You know it and I know it and so does everyone else. Please explain to me how he can get away with this and still keep his job."

"Well, first of all, you are not qualified to diagnose a drug problem, at least in the eyes of the law. Second, even if you called the police to arrest him, and even if we cooperated with them to catch Jeff in the act, he's entitled to due process in the courts. Also, arresting him doesn't automatically mean he loses his job. This company believes in a progressive disciplinary system, so Jeff is going to spend a lot of time with the employee assistance program to get drug education and treatment. Finally, he's a union employee, and he has an entire grievance and appeal process he can exercise."

"So we've got to take him back?"

"For now, with strict limitations that will protect everyone's health and safety. It won't make sense to trade one lawsuit for another."

Mark was quiet for a moment. "I'm going to lose some credibility with the rest of the crew over this, aren't I?"

"I'm sorry," said Janice. "Good luck—next time."

Mark is learning the hard way that being a manager can be frustrating and confusing. Like you, Mark is learning that situations are not nearly as clear-cut as they were before he was promoted.

You have probably bumped heads with someone by now over a similarly tough-to-resolve situation. Perhaps you, too, have been disappointed in some way with decisions or trade-offs or compromises someone else made for the greater good of the company. If you are bound by the company's labor contract, if the sales people can demand changes in your production schedule, or if senior management refuses to support your position on a contract dispute because of "political considerations," you naturally begin to wonder what your job is all about.

Just what role is the manager expected to play? Team leader? Coach? Social worker? Group facilitator? Policeman? Babysitter? All of the above, and more?

MEET THE NEW MANAGER
AND THE NEW WORKFORCE

Managers become necessary when businesses become larger. In very small businesses, the people doing the work can often manage themselves because everyone knows what everyone else is doing. Small business owners commonly wear all the hats to get all the work done: production manager, sales manager, financial manager, and research and development manager. Each time a new person joins the organization, however, the work to be done becomes a little more fragmented and communication becomes a little more complex. Soon, the company needs people who only manage.

This book describes all types of bosses—supervisors, chiefs, foremen, administrators, leadmen, department heads, district coordinators, and all the rest—as managers. They each perform the four roles or functions of management: planning, organizing, influencing, and facilitating. Over the years, these roles have remained the same, but *how* managers have fulfilled these roles has continued to change.

The traditional manager used to be the guy who simply carried out the orders of his boss. The thinking, deciding, and responsibility resided at the top of the organization and flowed downward, just like in the military services. The junior manager was no more and no less than an extension of the senior manager. Policy or procedure manuals attempted to prescribe the actions to be taken and the decisions to be made for every situation the manager might face.

This dependence on policies and procedures was comforting as long as the manager was only expected to carry out decisions made by someone else. The manuals were useful as long as there were only minimal changes from year to year. But as the marketplace became more competitive, and as new technologies changed the way people do business, managers' roles and responsibilities changed dramatically. In today's fast-moving marketplace, there isn't time to keep the procedure manuals up to date, even if they were still regarded as important; they would be out of date before the revisions could be agreed upon.

Today, managers still do the same four basic management functions: planning, organizing, influencing, and facilitating. But they do them in very different ways, usually within the context of empowered workers who are organized as formal and informal work teams.

Managers are still planning, but they no longer do it in isolation with manuals and charts; planning is done with lots of input from the work groups.

Organizing is no longer just scheduling; it's also training and facilitation of group discussion.

Influencing is more than telling and selling the dictums of a few senior managers; it requires team leadership, team promotion, training, mediation, consensus building, and more.

Facilitating is more than just controlling costs and errors; it reconciles actual performance with the expected performance specified in the planning function. Facilitating performance improvement is done with mutual trust among empowered workers, not recrimination; in most organizations, the "blame game" has most likely matured to fixing the problem, and not issuing the blame.

To succeed in your role in the 1990s, you must be a skilled communicator, innovator, decision maker, and problem solver. In a word, you are empowered to take more responsibility and accountability from those above you, whether you like it or not.

Chances are, there are fewer and fewer middle managers in your organization every year. This is because the rapid pace of change and other competitive pressures have forced most companies to thin the ranks of their middle- and upper-level managers. Many companies have endured a decade or more of soul-wrenching downsizing or rightsizing actions (corporate euphemisms for layoffs). They are loathe to let personnel costs start climbing again. It took them years to learn how to accomplish more with fewer managers at the top, but now that they've learned how to do it, there's no going back.

To avoid bureaucracy, these companies allow their managers to become more autonomous. Theoretically, this means that these leaner organizations can respond more effectively to the changing marketplace. This also means more and more management duties are pushed farther and farther down the management hierarchy.

The good news is that better decisions are probably being made by the lower-level managers who are closer to the facts and closer to the customers. You also are probably going to have more latitude to take risks and make decisions, simply because no one has the extra time to look over your shoulder and second-guess you.

In short, the traditional functions of the manager— planning, organizing, influencing, and facilitating—have stayed the same, but the manager's responsibilities have been vastly expanded. *What* you and other managers do hasn't really changed, but *how* you do it has changed dramatically. The new Performance Improvement Model (see Figure 2–1) illustrates the actual dynamics of the contemporary manager's job.

Your new responsibilities require you to spend more time planning and organizing the work to be done, and less time directly supervising the people doing the work. You need new skills to do this; even though you have been successful in

FIGURE 2–1
The Performance Improvement Model

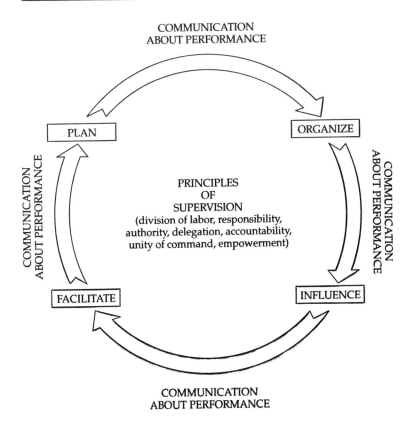

COMMUNICATION
ABOUT PERFORMANCE

PLAN

ORGANIZE

COMMUNICATION
ABOUT PERFORMANCE

COMMUNICATION
ABOUT PERFORMANCE

PRINCIPLES
OF
SUPERVISION
(division of labor, responsibility,
authority, delegation, accountability,
unity of command, empowerment)

FACILITATE

INFLUENCE

COMMUNICATION
ABOUT PERFORMANCE

the past because of your hands-on knowledge or because you were a capable administrator, your success as a manager will depend on your ability to really manage the efforts of others.

Your job no longer has clear starting points and ending points for your responsibilities. It is a fact of life that your job cannot be sharply defined or focused. One manager put it this way: "If there's a problem, and no one else claims it, it ends up on my desk."

Nor can your activities be easily predicted. You will be doing different tasks every day, although they can all be categorized in one of the four functions in the model. If you are most comfortable following orders, you may find this unsettling. For example, if you are told on Monday that you have the responsibility and authority to accomplish certain work, but then receive conflicting directions by Wednesday, you must respond quickly to update the work schedule and shift resources around to satisfy the new requests. Frankly, there just isn't any time to waste fretting or feeling frustrated.

Despite all of the aspects of your job you cannot control, you are not excused from doing your best. Don't let yourself become discouraged or cynical. With time, you'll learn to recognize your limits, your opportunities, and the difficult situations that you cannot do anything about. You know that you have many positive contributions to make. This is your opportunity to grow, make a larger difference in the company, change people's behaviors, and implement some of your new ideas. Can you make this new job more satisfying for yourself as long as you are in it? The sooner you become comfortable with your new roles, the better.

In the chapters to come, we'll take a closer look at the manager as a planner, organizer, influencer, and facilitator. In each case, these roles have been affected by trends that empower managers with more responsibility, accountability, and decision-making power. While the core functions remain the same, individual managers seem to be gaining an increasing amount of independence relative to how they perform these functions. This trend offers bright promises for organizations and their managers who can adapt and keep their business practices up to date.

So what if management has become a job requiring you to rely more on your judgment than on a policy or procedure manual? Happily, your nonmanagerial experience has probably prepared you to make many of these decisions. Your common sense, your sense of the company's values and priorities, and your instincts about your fellow employees further enhance your judgment.

Trusting and exercising her judgment was a problem for Rebecca, a new marketing manager. Her sales team sells electronic control products to various industries. She found that she was intimidated by the lack of structure in her department; what appeared to be freedom and flexibility when she was a salesperson looked and felt like a runaway train as a new manager.

Rebecca caught herself stalling her salespeople when they pressed her for decisions. Even worse, she no longer seemed to trust her creativity, so her ideas for sales promotion began to look stale and lifeless. Worse yet, she didn't know what to say when one of her struggling salespeople cautiously ventured an idea for a new product application. Finally, when the performance of her salespeople began to suffer, she forced herself to approach her manager.

Rebecca

I'm really uncomfortable making all these decisions. I'm afraid I'm going to fail or do something I'm not supposed to do. I'm paralyzed because I'm so worried about doing something wrong.

Rebecca's Manager

Your new job requires you to exercise judgment, Rebecca. The only mistake you're making is not trusting yours. The only situation I want to hear more about is the new product application—and that's only because I care about your salespersons and I want to spread good ideas like that to other parts of the company.

Rebecca

Some manager, huh? I want my people to be bold in the marketplace, but I know I sound timid and full of excuses in the sales meetings.

Rebecca's manager

Every other problem you've mentioned is within your authority and ability to handle. I obviously trust your judgment. You will, too, after a few mistakes and a few successes. I wish I could give you a book or a class that would guarantee success every time, but you know that our business changes too fast. This is on-the-job training, Becky, so get yourself a positive attitude, stop thinking so much about what might go wrong, and just do the best you can. I'll support you.

As a manager, Rebecca is a "knowledge worker"; her performance depends upon how well she uses her mind instead of how well she does production work. Information, quality, and customer service are her most powerful competitive tools, and these are the tools of the mind. No one can do her thinking for her. As a manager, she is expected to analyze the problem, talk to the appropriate people when necessary, solve the problems, and get the job done.

Rebecca, and most other workers under the age of 40, are different from older workers in several important ways. They are increasingly diverse in backgrounds, expectations, and abilities. They are increasingly more educated, mindful of the value of their work effort. They are also more sophisticated, often placing a high importance on the quality of their work life, their opportunities to develop themselves, and other intangible values such as achievement, prestige, independence, location, enjoyment, and self-realization.

Supervising this new type of worker requires you to adopt a management style stressing employee collaboration and participation. At least some of your employees want to be empowered to share in the running of the company. They want to work for a manager who shows respect for them by asking for their input and listening to their ideas.

With a shrinking pool of qualified labor, companies cannot afford to remain insensitive to their workers' wants and needs. Supervisors who see themselves as disciplinarians or watchdogs for the company are less common now because such old-fashioned management styles are not effective with the new types of workers.

In short, your job changes as quickly as your company changes. And why not? First-level and front-line managers frequently lead the process of change. Is your company facing increased competition? Is it struggling to keep up with new customer needs and new technologies? These pressures seem far away, but they affect your job because they force your company to make big changes frequently. If your company cannot adopt new technology that delivers more services for less cost, for example, or brings new products to market faster, sales will inevitably decline as customers seek better values elsewhere. Just as your subordinates want to contribute to solving your problems, you should be likewise looking for opportunities to contribute elsewhere, higher up in the organization. The odds are in your favor these days that your ideas will get serious consideration.

The following chart illustrates a useful way to think about how the roles of a manager have shifted during the past 10 to 15 years.

The Manager's Job Has Changed . . .

From	To
need for policies and procedures	need for high judgment tasks
activity orientation ("doing the right things")	results orientation ("achieving the right objectives")
dependence on technical skills	dependence on communication skills
high value placed on rigidity and constancy	high value placed on flexibility and responsiveness
control of workers	motivation of workers
narrow focus	broad focus
internal "us first" focus	external "customer first" focus
administrative skills	intrapreneurial skills
specific responsibilities	ambiguity, blurring of roles
static skill training	continuous learning
labor/management conflict	labor/management collaboration
management of white males by white males	management of diverse workforce by diverse managers
job security	risk, participation, career growth
the manager as disciplinarian	the manager as coach
people as parts of business	people as partners in business

THE MANAGER'S ROLES

Before you charge off to work, let's take another look at the new model of performance improvement (see Figure 2–1) and make it more usable for you in your new role.

If you haven't already done so, obtain a copy of your new job description from your supervisor or the human resources department. You may be told that it is incomplete or out of date, but study it anyway. It will reveal much about the scope of your new job.

Before you became a manager, your job was probably described as a group of activities worded something like the following:

"Process this many of those within that much time"

"Deliver . . ."

"Make . . ."

"Test . . ."

"Measure . . ."

"Write . . ."

And so on.

Now that you are one of the organization's leaders, the scope of your job is likely to be described in terms of results relating to the achievement of the organization's goals:

"Raise productivity by three percent . . ."

"Reduce absenteeism by 30 percent . . ."

"Reduce costs by nine percent . . ."

"Develop a scheduling system that allows us to reduce our inventory by 20 percent . . ."

And so on.

These may be called objectives, accountabilities, outputs, or something else in your organization, but the meaning is the same: Managers must focus on results. Briefly, your organization is asking you to get something done, and leaving it up to you to decide how to do it—within the rules and values of the organization, of course.

In other words, you are now responsible for improving the performance of those you supervise. What they do, and how well they do it, is within your control to influence, and therefore you are accountable for it. Their success, or lack of success, depends on you. In short, management is the promotion of ongoing performance improvement.

Look at it this way: Managers manage everything—people, projects, programs, and all the rest—by performing four traditional functions in the following sequence: planning, organizing, influencing, and facilitating. Everything a manager does relates to one or more of these functions; together, these functions make up the *management process*.

But it's even more accurate to describe the management process as the *performance management process* because the functions of management are meant to improve the organization's performance. By managing your employees' performance improvement process, you are contributing to the overall improvement of the organization's performance.

As you can see, two other components complete our new performance improvement model. The first component is the set of unwritten, natural laws of management that govern the interrelationships of people and groups of people within an organization. These are called the *principles of supervision*. Like it or not, these principles are the cultural and behavioral facts of life that guide our employees' expectations and responses. They always affect the four functions of management, so they are in the center of the model. We'll take a closer look at the principles of supervision in the next chapter.

The final component is *communication about performance*. Notice that all the functions of management are linked by communication about performance. These are the communication skills that help the manager talk about performance. Communicating about performance on an ongoing basis is necessary if the manager's efforts to plan, organize, influence, and facilitate performance improvement are ever going to be applied. For a discussion of how to communicate about performance, see Chapter 8, "Communicating about Performance."

Our four-function view of management has evolved in just the past 80-odd years (that's how young the art of management actually is; it's no wonder that it is still changing). The management process and the management functions that comprise it were first described in about 1910 by Henri Fayol, the managing director of a large coal mine in France. He saw the organization as a body—the "body corporate." Fayol viewed the activities of every business organization fitting into six functions: technical (production), commercial (buying, selling, and exchange), financial (finding and employing capital), security (protection of people and property), accounting, and managerial (planning, organization, command, coordination, and control). All of these functions of a business were well understood, according to Fayol, except the managerial function, which he believed was mingled with the other functions.

Fayol's writings did much to clarify the unique relationships and contributions of the management functions as they relate to the rest of the organization, and he is now generally regarded as the "father of modern management." His five-function management model has been modified dozens of times since then to arrive at the four functions portrayed in Figure 2–1.

What do these models teach us? In the first place, management is not an activity with a distinct beginning and a definite end. It is an ongoing cycle that repeats itself again and again for everything and everyone the manager manages. The sequence in which the functions are performed never varies. A manager will be at different places in the cycle with each situation, of course, but he or she will always be planning before organizing, influencing before facilitating, and so on.

Management is distinct from all the other activities of an enterprise, yet it is not an isolated activity, separate from the other activities of the organization. Rather, it is directly and deeply involved in activities like production, marketing, finance, and every other activity of the company. Management work is not the money-making work of the organization; rather, it maintains the successful operation of all the other activities that do the work of the business.

As we discussed in Chapter 1, many managers do not understand the difference between doing the work and

managing the work. Some chairpersons, foremen, data processing supervisors, customer service coordinators, group
leaders, generals, deans, principals, program directors, medical directors, head nurses, managing editors, sales managers,
chief engineers, controllers, partners in accounting firms, and
countless others in management jobs are too deeply im-
mersed in the work of their organization to be effective managers. They do not understand that their responsibilities to
plan, organize, influence, and facilitate are critical to maintaining the organization and moving it towards its goals.

The management process is a dynamic activity, constantly
changing in response to circumstances and opportunities.
How much of the following management functions do you
expect to do?

Planning is the process of determining in advance what
should be accomplished and how it should be done. When a
manager plans, he or she visualizes the future direction of the
work group's effort. A good plan always states an objective
and specifies the time and resources needed to accomplish the
objective.

For example, the manager of a warehouse crew anticipates
the needs to receive and stack new merchandise, load the current orders, and count the inventory. To accomplish these objectives, he must plan accordingly. He must have the right
tools on hand (forklifts, clipboards, and calculators), schedule
enough time to complete the tasks (a day? a week?), and
make the necessary adjustments in the work assignments
(how many people will be needed?).

Organizing is the process of assigning people and allocating
resources to accomplish the objectives set in the planning
process. This means having qualified people and the resources they need in the right place at the right time so the organization can succeed. The warehouse manager in the
example above must organize a crew of the right size and
skill to do the tasks he has planned, and they must have the
necessary equipment available when they need it.

When the planned objectives are not met, a manager may
decide to reorganize. Are the people doing the inventory

showing up too early, before the current orders have been filled and before the new merchandise has been stocked? The manager has the power to change the organization to find a different combination of people and resources that will be more productive. He or she may change the work flow, reassign workers to new supervisors, buy new equipment, or physically rearrange the workplace. He may change formal relationships, such as having the inventory people take direction from the stocking foreman, or promote informal relationships, such as having the leaders of the work groups assign "aisle captains," if he thinks it will help get the work done in a better way.

Influencing is the process of determining or affecting the behavior of others. Managers seek to persuade employees to view their personal objectives as linked to the attainment of the corporate objectives. "What's good for the company is good for all of us" is the message the employees have to understand. Using motivation and leadership, the manager strives to maximize the employee's abilities on behalf of the company. The ability to influence an employee depends on the manager's interpersonal communication skills.

Facilitating, the fourth and final management function, means identifying gaps in performance between that which was planned and that which was actually accomplished, and then working with empowered workers to raise performance to meet expectations. Effective facilitation provides accurate and timely feedback about performance that can be used to update the organization's plans.

The planning function does not become credible until there is an organization that can implement the plan. Likewise, effective organization is just a theory until the employees are actually motivated to do the work. Influence depends on the facilitation function to keep the work effort channeled. Facilitation to close performance gaps leads to updated plans. Finally, all of the functions are integrated by communication skills focused on improving performance.

In the next chapter, we will look at the principles of supervision. These are the unwritten rules that guide managers.

Chapter Three

The Principles of Supervision

Why do organizations continue to function more or less smoothly, in spite of the inevitable conflicts, pressures, and changes to which they are subjected? How can they continue to process and build and ship and sell day after day without breaking down? Are there unwritten rules or concepts that explain the invisible bonds holding organizations together?

Yes, there are principles and concepts that serve as the glue holding organizations together. These are unwritten rules, or natural laws as some refer to them, that explain how and why a group of people continue to work together toward a common goal. They are not inviolate, but they do reflect the aspects of human nature that draw us to organizations and keep us working toward the group's success.

DIVISION OF LABOR

The concept of division of labor, also called the specialization of labor, was introduced earlier as a way to determine the functions of an organization. When organizing a group of people for the first time, it is a useful way of thinking about matching the people to the tasks at hand.

By subdividing all activities into their most basic tasks, managers can be certain of who is responsible for what. They can also write more specific and measurable job descriptions.

A foreman on a building maintenance crew, for example, applies the division of labor principle to assign floor polishing, wall painting, duct cleaning, and other jobs. If everyone does his or her job, the building will be cleaned and painted on schedule.

You may see this principle in action first-hand as a "who's doing what" problem. Some of your more experienced people will know a lot about the jobs of other people. Perhaps they started in the department as a media planner or oiler or payroll clerk; perhaps they were cross-trained to take over for people on vacation; or perhaps they just picked it up because they've grown with the department. These people are obviously very valuable contributors, but what do you do when they want to be involved in everyone else's jobs?

When people wander afield from their jobs, confusion and misunderstandings can escalate quickly. You start to hear angry voices saying things like, "Whose job is this, anyway?" and "Mind your own business!" True, the seasoned pro may be able to do his co-workers' jobs better than they can, but he can't do them all.

If you have a person who has clearly stopped being a supportive resource to the team and is instead interfering in the tasks normally performed by others with the masquerade of helping them, watch out. You have a powerful cannon loose on your deck. You cannot afford to alienate him, but you have to rein him in or you will be stuck with a meddler who is forever slowing down other employees with suggestions they don't want or need.

This person needs to be redirected back to his assignment. If you discover he's bored, give him some real challenges that need his expertise. If he's unable to do his job, and therefore feels compelled to do others' jobs, get him some help. Say to him, "Sure, you can do that job better. You can do lots of other jobs around here, too, and when we ask for your help, we're grateful for your expertise. But your job right now is over here, and we need you to get it done." You must assert the principle of division of labor to prevent confusion in the ranks about who is doing what.

RESPONSIBILITY

Responsibility is an obligation to perform work activities. Once we have made a commitment to accept responsibility for a task, it is our natural inclination to work to fulfill it. If we accept responsibility, we expect to receive penalties or rewards commensurate with our performance.

Responsibilities are shared in an organization. They are delegated, assumed, avoided, passed on to someone else, and otherwise distributed. The concept of responsibility gives employees their focus; it also enriches their work life with intangible benefits such as self-esteem, job satisfaction, and the respect and praise of their peers. If you assume the responsibility for a company-owned fast-food restaurant, for example, it becomes in a very real sense "your" shop: you plan for the grand opening, organize for long-term operations, influence the employees by motivating them and instilling in them the proper attitude about customer service, and control the operations with proper accounting, training, and quality control procedures.

When responsibilities are unclear, the organization suffers because the work does not get done. Ironically, the simplest tasks often do not get the attention they need. If a task is not specifically mentioned in a person's job description, it is a potential problem. Nonroutine projects are particularly troublesome because every detail has to be assigned to someone. Everyone even remotely involved in a project has the responsibility to help the group by asking, "Who is taking care of this?" Whenever you raise this question, you save yourself from a future headache.

Safety and quality are commonly lost in the category of "everyone's responsibility." Since everyone is responsible, no one is responsible—except someone else! The prudent manager recognizes this and assigns primary responsibility to a quality control specialist or a safety engineer.

The nuclear power plant accident at Three Mile Island, Pennsylvania, in 1979 is an example of how dangerous a situation can be when responsibilities are not clear. Public safety was jeopardized when radioactive gas was released, exposing the citizens in the nearby communities to high levels of radioactivity. A study of the incident revealed that important safety steps had been overlooked and omitted, partially due to confusion about who was responsible for which procedures. Bridge construction, drug formulation, product packaging, auto manufacturing, and most other businesses have their own versions of this potential problem. The remedy is to acknowledge the confusion and document each worker's responsibilities.

AUTHORITY

The companion principle to responsibility is authority, defined as the right to decide, to direct others to take action, or to perform certain duties in the process of achieving organizational goals. It is called a companion principle because responsibility and the authority to take the actions necessary to fulfill the responsibility are usually conferred at the same time.

In other words, if a person accepts the responsibility to increase sales by 15 percent, for example, he or she will need the authority to hire and fire salespeople, make pricing decisions, target new customers, spend money on product promotion, and perform similar activities. Managers should be mindful that responsibility without authority is doomed to fail.

DELEGATION

The process of assigning responsibility along with the related authority is called delegation. This is one of the key concepts of management and it is central to your need to accomplish objectives through the efforts of others.

A manager unwilling or unable to delegate is limited to the amount of work he or she is able to do alone. Delegation enables a manager to accomplish more challenging jobs because it extends the manager's capabilities, multiplying the efforts directed towards an objective. Through delegation, for example, a manager can assemble a team of people with specialized talents to focus on a problem.

Delegating does not pass on the ultimate responsibility for the success or failure of an assignment, however. Delegating is an option, another way to get things done, but the final responsibility remains with the manager who made the assignment. You cannot excuse yourself by saying, "It's not my fault. I gave that job to Bob and Julie, and they really messed up." If the wrong person was selected to handle the job, or if the person was not furnished with the required resources, the manager must accept the blame. The manager is likewise entitled to the credit if his or her decisions to delegate prove to be correct and the work is completed successfully.

The following are among the most important reasons to delegate.

Delegation may result in faster decisions. Upward delegation to supervisors occurs when subordinates do not trust the supervisors to support decisions made at lower levels. "Kicking it upstairs" for a decision can lead to time-consuming bottlenecks.

Delegation may lead to better decisions. The employees closest to the job are usually in an excellent position to solve problems and initiate positive changes.

Delegation is a means of developing leadership, planning, and organizing skills in subordinates by giving them opportunities to demonstrate their capabilities. How will you ever know how much an employee can handle unless you start trusting him or her? When challenged by the right assignment, a subordinate can learn by doing.

Delegation may improve motivation. Employees who feel they have the trust and confidence of management may work harder to justify that trust and live up to heightened expectations.

Delegation may also improve morale. When you trust your employees, you can expect a positive attitude in return. Furthermore, delegation confers a sense of ownership of assigned tasks on subordinates, so they may take more pride in their work.

ACCOUNTABILITY

After an assignment has been delegated and the responsibility and authority have been passed on, the manager is held accountable for the results of his or her decisions and actions. Accountability is any means of ensuring that the person who is supposed to do a task actually performs it and does so correctly. It is a part of the control function and becomes important after a task is completed.

Accountability cannot be passed on by the manager. Part of it can be shared with subordinates, but in the end, the highest-level managers are held accountable for the success or failure of the organization.

Yes, the buck really does stop with you!

UNITY OF COMMAND

The unity of command principle is the belief that each person should only be accountable to one supervisor; in other words, each person should have only one boss. This simplifies communication and discipline by eliminating potentially contradictory orders from more than one manager.

In companies organized in traditional ways, the unity of command principle is clear. It is a bit more ambiguous in some organizations that adopt a more flexible approach.

Margaret (the manager of the MIS department)

Unity of command is a useful carryover from traditional organizations. It even works here, in a modified form, where we've got something called a "matrix" organization.

I have a lot of people out on loan to other departments, so at any one time, they have two managers: a project manager who runs the department they are assigned to, and a functional manager—me—at the same time.

Margaret's new employee

So who's really my boss?

This is a potentially troubling question for a worker. Beyond the confusion over whom he or she takes orders from, the possibility of mischief—playing one manager against the other—exists. Sometimes, each manager assumes the other manager is holding the employee accountable when, in fact, neither of them do.

Margaret provides a clear solution. "Here's how I keep this from becoming confusing: I think of the department manager as a customer—you know, a real customer, just like someone outside the company, who has certain needs that we are trying to satisfy. The assignment for any employee in my department then becomes very clear: to meet the customer's needs.

"I imagine my people getting into an imaginary repair truck every morning and driving out to service the customer, even though this all takes place within our building here. Sure, I expect to hear from my employees when they have a problem, need advice, or finish the assignment, but the other manager calls the shots on the job because he's the customer.

"The value of a matrix organization is considerable—it's generally more efficient, requires less time to make a decision, and does a better job of satisfying internal and external customers. But if we didn't apply an updated version of the unity of command principle, we would lose all those benefits in the resulting chaos.

"The challenge for all of us—the employee and both managers— is to appreciate that the employee has different bosses at different times for different reasons. While he's on assignment, meeting the needs of the second manager, my employee is beyond the practical limits of my supervision. Why pretend otherwise? Even though he is literally sitting at the next desk, I cannot effectively manage him as he works through his tasks, unless, of course, I begin looking over his shoulder every few minutes and second-guessing his decisions. That would clearly get in the way of getting the work done. If I don't trust him, I shouldn't delegate to him; and if the problem is my paranoia that someone is going to decide something without me, I have too much time to worry!

"The second manager can't fire my employee; nor is she responsible for his training and development, performance reviews, or compensation decisions. As an internal customer, I welcome her feedback on my employee's performance, but when the assignment is finished, the matrix changes and she's no longer one of my employee's bosses."

SPAN OF CONTROL

How many people does your company think a manager can effectively manage?

Span of control is the reach or spread of a manager's effective influence over his direct reports (those subordinates who report directly to him). The span of control principle acknowledges that day-to-day management requires some of the manager's time and effort for each and every subordinate.

If Jennifer's manager does not have the time to directly plan her development and assignments, organize her resources, influence her behavior, or provide meaningful controls, Jennifer will be poorly managed. Left to decide her own priorities and monitor her own performance, she may or may not get her work done properly.

A span of control that is too broad or too thin almost always costs the organization time and money. The near-term costs include lost efficiency, low productivity, and wasted materials. The long-term costs are the compounded costs of a poorly directed employee plus the additional recruitment costs to find and train Jennifer's replacement. That's right: a broad span of control usually means higher employee turnover. This is logical, considering that most people want to have some personal attention from their manager in the form of feedback, direction, and personal development planning.

Take away the individual attention of the manager, and the employee begins to feel like just an impersonal cog in the organization, not cared about or valued.

Span of control is set by each organization's policy and is easily portrayed in the organizational chart. It specifies who reports to whom and how many other people also report to that same person.

Traditionally organized companies have held their span of control to 10 employees or less. But your company may be more progressive; it may be seeking new ways of expanding each manager's span of control.

Broader spans of control are necessary when there are few middle managers. Sometimes this type of organization is described as flat because there are not very many levels on the organizational chart. Broad spans of control are workable when the organization has a culture that empowers its employees, which is the final principle of supervision we'll discuss.

EMPOWERMENT

Empowerment—which is also described in its various forms as powersharing, shared decision making, and participatory management—is a corporate value that is becoming a principle of supervision. Driven by the economic necessity to thin their managerial ranks during the 1980s, many companies discovered that their employees could, in fact, be trusted to accomplish specific objectives. All that was required on the part of the organization was to treat their employees with respect and patience as they learned to self-manage themselves. As you will see in Chapter 7, the most effective approach to facilitating the closure of performance gaps is to empower workers.

Some organizations have embraced this concept in a wholesale fashion, extending it to self-managed work teams that function effectively with only nominal oversight from a traditional-looking manager. Such an empowered work team assumes all the managerial chores, including scheduling, ordering materials, selecting vendors, hiring and firing personnel, and budgeting, just to name a few. Keep this in perspective, however: while over half of all the companies in the United States with more than 100 employees in 1992 were experimenting with some variation of formally organized, self-directed work teams, only about five percent of all employees were actually participating in the teams.

Empowerment is being used in almost every organization in some form, either formally or informally. You may hear this buzzword frequently, so try to get your company's definition. Ask your manager how your company views employee empowerment; is this approach formally applied or officially endorsed? If your company is using it, or beginning to use it, there are likely to be ample training materials made available to you that explain your organization's approach.

In the next chapter, we'll examine the first of the four functions of management: planning.

The Principles of Supervision at Work

Division of labor	means	"Let's divide the work among us."
Responsibility	means	"I (or you) own this job; you can hold me accountable for it."
Authority	means	"I (or you) get to decide how this is going to get done."
Delegation	means	"You have the responsibility and authority to accomplish this assignment."
Accountability	means	"The buck stops here."
Unity of command	means	"No matter whom else you work with, you are accountable to only one person."
Span of control	means	"There are limits to how many people a manager can effectively manage."
Empowerment	means	"I trust you to perform these functions and accomplish these results; this means much more than just delegating a task to you."

Chapter Four

Planning Skills

Before a manager does anything, he or she must plan. The manager's plans provide the framework for what does and doesn't happen in the organization. Plans that are practical yield positive results: satisfied customers, high employee morale, and enough profits to fund the company's growth. On the other hand, poor planning leads to late deliveries, rush schedules that require expensive overtime interspersed with idle machines or workers with nothing to do, inefficient duplication of work, and quarreling and excuse making among the employees.

AN OVERVIEW OF PLANNING

Good plans specify work priorities and how the work will be done. They answer the twin questions, "What work is really important to do now?" and "How are we going to get it done?" A plan is ready to be communicated to the people who will implement it only when it states an objective and specifies the time and resources needed to accomplish the objective.

To people being supervised, a manager's role in the planning process may appear to begin and end in his or her department. Actually, every manager makes a contribution to the umbrella corporate planning process by regularly communicating with other members of the management team.

Long-range plans, mid-range plans, and short-range plans fit into a hierarchy of planning that mirrors the management hierarchy. One of the chief advantages of the planning process is the elimination of conflicting plans, cross-purposes between departments, and inefficiency. The plans of each manager must support the overall goals that give the organization its direction.

THE BENEFITS OF PLANNING

By planning well, a manager can obtain important benefits for his or her organization. Planning is active, not passive; it causes the planners to shed their "wait and see" attitudes about the future by forcing them to forecast the environment of the future. By imagining what their problems and opportunities will be next month or next year, managers can prepare the organization's best responses. Planning almost always saves time and money.

Planning also gives a company direction in the form of objectives. Based on the "what if" scenarios they forecast, managers know what they can and cannot realistically achieve over a given period of time. Knowing this helps set day-to-day goals and reduces costly shifts in policy and strategy. Another benefit is the sense of teamwork that is fostered when the corporate goals are communicated throughout the company in the form of a plan.

Finally, planning yields valuable insights into the company's problems and opportunities. It is no coincidence that companies that plan are almost always holding favorable positions relative to their competitors. They are able to stay one step ahead because they plan. To plan is to predict change.

Planning is no guarantee of success, however. No one can forecast the future and make all the necessary decisions in advance. Precious little in the marketplace is predictable, and even less can be controlled with certainty. In spite of the ambiguities of the future, though, planning usually does help everyone in the organization function more effectively.

When I plan, I . . .

(1 = rarely, 2 = occasionally, 3 = sometimes, 4 = frequently, 5 = almost always)

_____ Finish on time.

_____ Write my plan down.

_____ Refer to my plan and make mid-term corrections.

_____ Keep my plan in sight.

_____ Communicate my plan to others.

_____ Anticipate obstacles.

_____ Prepare a backup plan.

_____ Delegate.

_____ Set deadlines for myself and others.

_____ Keep track of where my time is spent.

_____ Keep in mind the value of my time.

_____ Focus on those activities that will have the greatest impact.

_____ Review my list of goals.

_____ Have a clear idea of what I want to accomplish next week.

_____ Set priorities according to importance, not urgency.

_____ Isolate myself for quiet thinking time.

_____ Focus on results, not just activities.

_____ Keep the organization's mission and goals in mind.

_____ Reward myself for meeting my plan.

_____ Total

Add your points. If your total is less than 60, you need significant development of your planning skills.

TYPES OF PLANS

The planning for which management is responsible can be described as long-term planning, mid-term planning, and operational planning. They all serve the same purpose: essentially, they are the manager's compass to his or her priorities. You are not responsible for all of these plans, but you have to be aware of them so your contributions to the planning process fit with the others.

Your company's long-term plan looks forward three to five years and beyond. This is called a strategic plan because it focuses on strategy, and it addresses the fundamental questions of the company's mission: What is the nature of our business? Are we correct to stay in this business? What long-term trends are likely to affect our customers or ourselves, and how will those trends affect us? How must we change to maintain or improve our competitive advantage, and what must we do to prepare for those changes? What should this company be doing differently five years from now? How should it be performing financially? The strategic plan usually includes a mission statement that answers the questions, What is our core business? and What do we ultimately hope to achieve with it? As a new manager, you will have little effect on the strategic plan, but you should know what it is and be able to communicate it to your employees. Ask your manager or human resources department for a copy of it.

Mid-term planning looks forward one to three years and focuses on how to compete in a particular industry or market segment. These mid-term, tactical plans are subsets of the long-term plan, addressing many of the same issues within the context of a competitive marketplace. Typical questions asked of a mid-range plan are: What changes are going to occur among our customers, suppliers, and competitors, and how must we change to prepare for this new environment? What skills will our personnel need to compete effectively, and what must we do now so that they will be ready? A popular model for this analysis is the S.W.O.T. Analysis developed by the Harvard Business School, which asks managers to list the company's Strengths, Weaknesses, Opportunities, and Threats.

Operational plans focus on the work that must be done within the next 12 months. These day-to-day, week-to-week plans are concerned with current levels of staffing, the implementation of the marketing plan, vendor reliability, and customer satisfaction, among many other issues. Operational planners ask "How?" and "When?" more often than they ask "What should we be doing next?" and "Why are we doing this?"

The hierarchy of plans is addressed by a hierarchy of managers. Most senior managers do the long-range planning and the lower-level managers supervise the day-to-day operational plans. As you can see in Figure 4–1, the most progressive organizations have mechanisms that facilitate frank and dynamic discussion and feedback between the different levels of management. Communication between the people making the plans and the people implementing the plans improves everyone's performance and the overall productivity of the organization.

If plans are for nonrepetitive activities like promotion programs, project development, and budgets, they are further categorized as *single-use plans*. Repetitive activities governed by policies, standard procedures, and rules are called *standing plans*.

HOW TO WRITE A GOOD PLAN

Successful managers plan to plan—and then do it.

Planning is the process of determining in advance what should be accomplished and how it should be done. It is a three-step process:

Step 1: Decide what your priorities are. Define the few large goals that will guide the rest of the planning process, keeping in mind where you are in relation to the goals right now.

Step 2: Develop the midpoint objectives that will support the goals, taking into consideration the barriers and aids that exist in the environment.

Step 3: Divide each objective into simple action plans that will lead to the accomplishment of the objectives and the goals.

FIGURE 4-1
Types of Plans

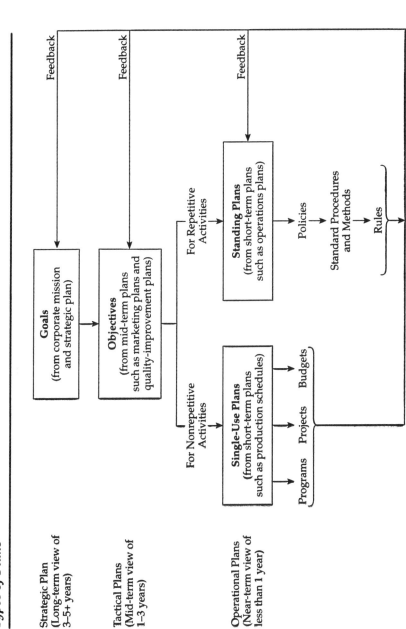

FIGURE 4–2
The Planning Process

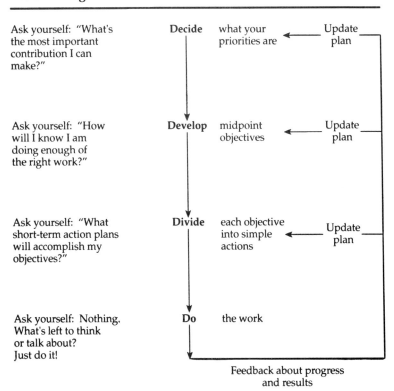

| Ask yourself: "What's the most important contribution I can make?" | **Decide** | what your priorities are | Update plan |

| Ask yourself: "How will I know I am doing enough of the right work?" | **Develop** | midpoint objectives | Update plan |

| Ask yourself: "What short-term action plans will accomplish my objectives?" | **Divide** | each objective into simple actions | Update plan |

| Ask yourself: Nothing. What's left to think or talk about? Just do it! | **Do** | the work |

Feedback about progress
and results

Specificity is the key to making a plan successful. For example, a goal that simply states that a company wants "to grow" is doomed to remain on the wish list. What kind of growth would satisfy this goal? Financial, personnel, market share, number of product categories? Something else? Without more specific direction, the employees of this company are probably going to grow in different directions. Oh, they'll be busy all right, but they probably won't be doing the same things or the right things. At best, they will stay out of each other's way; more likely, they will sooner or later be in conflict because they will be competing for the company's limited resources.

Or think about an objective or goal that says nothing more than "to improve the company's productivity." What does this mean? Does it mean cut back to reduce expenses, or does it mean expand the business with the 25 most profitable accounts? Perhaps it means neither, but no one will know until it is too late, after the time and money are misspent. We'll discuss how to write good objectives later in this chapter.

CHARACTERISTICS OF GOOD PLANS

Successful plans are specific, but they are also flexible. A good manager has a "best case" plan that is used if and when a situation unfolds as hoped. He or she also has a "worst case" plan to fall back on when the original plan is upset by surprise circumstances. Between the best case and the worst case plan lies the "target plan," the one that will probably reflect the actual situation. The prudent manager watches carefully for signs of how well the target plan is working, and then adjusts accordingly, perhaps by hiring a new advertising agency, increasing production, or canceling orders for raw materials.

Good planning reflects reality. The objective writing exercise is a formal way of asking: Is this result really attainable? If the success of a delivery service hinges on getting the average order delivered within 35 minutes of the customer's phone call, and the drivers' best average has been 42 minutes, the objective may be unrealistic. Simply wanting a change to occur is not enough to make it happen.

Plans should also reflect the skills, knowledge, and attitudes of the people implementing the plans. In the case noted above, perhaps the delivery people are unfamiliar with the streets of the city and routinely have to consult their maps. If that is their level of skill and knowledge, the manager of the delivery service must take this into account. If they have never performed the desired activity successfully at the standard set by the objective, they cannot be expected to do so without making changes that make the new performance possible. Do they need some kind of training? Do they need two-way radios or mobile phones in their vehicles? Should they be strategically located in advance throughout the city? Can they improve their response time if assigned to smaller geographic areas?

If the manager is committed to the new performance objective, he or she must come up with a workable plan that will make the change happen.

Good plans should state specific ways to achieve the desired results. In the case of the delivery service above, the manager may plan on meeting the target of 35 minutes by reorganizing the route map, putting phones in all the cars, and providing additional training to the drivers. If an objective is supported by reasonable and specific actions like these that make the objective possible to achieve, the objective should be given a chance to succeed.

Finally, plans have to be communicated upward and downward in the organization's hierarchy. The delivery drivers cannot be held accountable for new levels of performance if the plans are not communicated to them. Also, the manager may not expect the support of senior management when asked for more money to buy the phones if they do not understand or accept the plan.

HOW TO WRITE GOOD OBJECTIVES

One of the truisms among managers is, "Good direction yields good results." If managers expect to obtain optimal results through the efforts of their employees, they must make the extra effort to communicate their precise expectations to those employees.

Objectives and goals are the mechanisms that clearly link a plan to the actions that make it a reality. The process of writing objectives down forces us to think through the steps we'll have to take in order to accomplish the objective. This is more than mental exercise; by breaking down the large tasks required of us into simple actions, the difficulty of the tasks is diminished.

It is the manager's responsibility to establish clear and specific goals, objectives, and action plans. Such objectives should:

1. State a clear purpose ("In order to increase productivity by 10 percent, . . .").
2. Be measurable (". . . assemble 50 additional television sets . . .").
3. Specify a time frame within which they will be achieved (". . . every eight-hour shift . . .").
4. Specify the resources needed (". . . by operating an additional assembly line for subassemblies . . .").
5. Specify the quality of the output (". . . without increasing the rate of rejects above two percent . . .")
6. Be challenging but also attainable.
7. Be expressed in writing to increase commitment and understanding while reducing confusion.

The more specific an objective is, the more likely it is to be accomplished. By quantifying how much will be done, when it will be finished, and who will do it using which resources, the plan leaves less possibility of misunderstanding or error. Figure 4–3 suggests a format for writing clear, workable objectives.

HOW TO WRITE GOOD ACTION PLANS

If the objectives are precisely stated and quantified, they will provide clear direction to the people actually doing the work. Clear objectives lead to clear work plans, also called *activity plans* or *action plans*. Objectives state what must be done; action plans expand on the details of the activities to explain how it will be done. An objective is typically no longer than a paragraph, but an action plan can be many pages in length. An action plan can be thought of as a plan within a plan that specifies all the work details that must be identified, assigned, and accomplished.

FIGURE 4-3
Objective-Setting Worksheet

What's the action? (verb)	What's the result? (noun)	When's it due? (time frame)	Who will check? (monitor)	What's the purpose? (reason/purpose)

For each objective, how will you know you're making progress?

Indicators (activity)	When's it due? (time frame)

The best way to write an action plan is to imagine doing the work, step-by-step, and then write down the key details. The following 10-point checklist describes the action planning process for a moderately complex project.

1. List everything that must be done to accomplish the objective.
2. List the tasks to be done in the order they should be finished.
3. Identify by name who will be doing which tasks.
4. List the resources that will be necessary for the completion of each task.
5. Note the time needed for each task, including the estimated delivery time needed for materials not already on hand.
6. Consider the constraints that might upset this plan and note the steps that can be taken to avoid them.
7. Write the plan on a chart that reflects the passage of time such as an event calendar or a time-line chart that shows the appropriate beginning and ending points of every activity (sometimes called a Gantt chart).
8. Identify the control points that will mark the progress of activity.
9. Develop a back-up plan just in case you cannot accomplish the objective, finish the action plan, or are only partially successful.
10. Update the plan periodically to reflect feedback and the most current data.
11. Refer to the plan frequently. Make it a dynamic part of your operations. It is actually easier to write a plan than to follow it!

Plans that are successful, regardless of their level in the hierarchy, specify what or how much should be accomplished and when the work will be done. A plan is ready to be communicated to the people who will implement it only when clear, measurable objectives are supported by well-reasoned action plans.

MANAGEMENT BY OBJECTIVES

Objectives are proven to be very useful in the measurement and control of planning and performance. In fact, the practice of directing an organization with objectives has matured during the past two decades into a formal management style called management by objectives or MBO.

Management by objectives is a process in which supervisors and subordinates identify common goals, agree on objectives that specify how the subordinate will contribute to the accomplishment of the goals, and agree to use the measured results to evaluate the subordinate's performance.

The structure and guidelines of the MBO approach forces managers to communicate with each other about difficult subjects that might otherwise be left to chance. It also forces managers to plan explicitly instead of simply responding to opportunities and crisis as they arise.

MBO is a more systematic and rational approach to management than crisis management, fire fighting, or "seat-of-the-pants" methods. It is also different from reactive or reflexive management approaches because it focuses on achieving measurable results. Philosophically, it is results oriented, and it uses mutually agreed-upon objectives and performance measures as the primary basis of motivation, evaluation, and control efforts.

Here is how an MBO program works. Imagine you are the manager of the data processing (DP) department. You must meet with your employees to discuss and set the department's goals, which in this case are changing because of the number of microcomputers being purchased for use throughout the company, including your department.

It is reasonable to assume that the role of the DP department will change because many of the routine reports will soon be generated without involvement from your DP staff. In essence, your department is becoming less of a batch processing operation and more of a microcomputer support resource.

So what will the new goals look like? They will probably identify new customer service needs and new competencies

FIGURE 4–4
The Management by Objective (MBO) Process

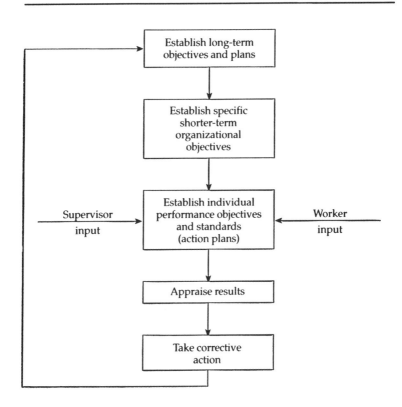

for technical support people, for example. Communicating the new goals of the department to your employees will probably require several lengthy discussions.

Next, you and your employees suggest objectives that will support the attainment of the agreed-upon goals. In this case, completely new objectives must be written to help the department fulfill its new role as a support resource for microcomputer users. The current objectives that relate to batch processing assignments probably need to be updated or scrapped. What else? Are any new technical training programs needed? Together, you and your workers decide upon the following:

• What the employees will do.
• How soon these tasks will be done.
• What resources or approaches will be used.
• How the employees' performances will be measured.
• When to meet next so the plan can be evaluated.

A great advantage of the MBO process is the access to the decision-making process it provides for employees low on the corporate ladder. This has two distinct benefits. First, it gives each employee some control over his or her work plan. This heightens the employee's commitment to the objectives and enhances the likelihood that the objectives will be accomplished. Second, the company receives the benefits of the employee's input, which may include the most accurate descriptions of situations that relate to the objectives and new suggestions for improving productivity that management might not have considered. Of course, the MBO process may also result in a higher morale among the workforce.

The dynamics of the MBO process are illustrated in Figure 4-4. Notice that the process begins with strong support and commitment from upper management. MBO depends on enthusiastic participation by employees at all levels of the company; after all, they are the ones who make the extra effort to communicate and make the process work. If senior management does not genuinely trust the subordinates or believe the MBO process is worth the commitment, the wrong attitude will be communicated and cripple the process.

You will notice that the MBO process does for the individual what the planning process does for the company. The MBO action plans translate the corporate goals and objectives into performance objectives and standards for individuals. Just like in the companywide planning process, specificity as to what is to be done and when it is to be completed is crucial.

Critics of the MBO approach caution that some employees are not ready to participate in the building of their own action plans. Some people tend to overcommit to what they can do. They are anxious to please and sincerely believe in their optimistic forecasts, but such forecasts may be unrealistic. For example, if a production engineer commits to doubling the number of drawings he will complete in the next three months and no substantive changes have been made in his other assignments to make this possible, he has set himself up to fail. This engineer's manager should counsel him to think more about how the higher output will be attained, and then help him set a more realistic figure. If this coaching and counseling does not occur in an atmosphere that promotes trust, the employee will lose confidence in the process and stop participating actively.

Critics of the MBO process have also voiced concern about the difficulty of setting meaningful goals, about excessive paperwork, about excessive requirements to maintain the system, and about a tendency in some companies to focus too much on the short-term plans at the expense of the long-term plans.

Nevertheless, the general consensus is that MBO is an excellent model for planning. Many employees and managers may not need a formal planning system all the time, but most find the MBO principles of specificity, measurement, and written action plans an excellent way to avoid misunderstandings and inefficiencies.

Furthermore, the MBO approach is also generally acknowledged as one of the best tools for monitoring the results of the company's plans. The objectives force managers and their workers to communicate their expectations for performance, so monitoring performance becomes much more straightforward. The workers should be able to know just how well they are doing at any time, without involving the manager, thereby empowering them with more self-management. This is a move away from subjective performance evaluations and is generally regarded as a more equitable and quicker way to identify performance problems.

WHY PLANS FAIL

They are unrealistic. If expectations are unrealistic to begin with, the plan is doomed. Since we naturally want to please the people who are important to us, especially our boss, we may develop a tendency to agree too quickly to perform impossible tasks. Assuring a co-worker you can do something just because you know that he wants to hear "just the good news" compounds your error in judgment: not only will you fail to deliver as promised, but you will be labeled as an unreliable performer who cannot plan well. His unrealistic requests stop being his problem the moment you say, "Yes, I can do that." Once you agree to make the commitment, the unrealistic expectations become *your* problem.

If you find you are falling into a pattern of making unrealistic plans, stop making commitments until you learn new ways of getting the critical information you are clearly lacking and learn to say no to unrealistic requests.

They do not take the team into account. How many of us have fantasized a plan involving our team members without seeking their input? It's common sense: If we want someone to join our plan, we have to make sure of the following:

- The person is willing to participate and own his fair share.
- The person is capable and has the skills and the time to participate.
- The person is not in conflict with other priorities.

They lack meaningful checkpoints. Nearly as failure-prone are the plans that allow planners to postpone making the tough decisions. Our natural tendency is to keep all our options open as long as we can, but failing to decide can be very costly. The way to avoid this trap is to commit to periodic reviews of the plan, up front and in writing, while you are still objective and looking at the plan from a distance.

For example, you may specify in your plan that if you fail to meet your sales goals, then you will begin closing sales offices, no matter what. It's no guarantee, but when your own plan in your own handwriting specifies that you will make such-and-such a decision on such-and-such a date, and you know that you wrote that plan when you were a lot more objective than you are now, you're more likely to follow your own good advice and stick to the plan.

They fail to provide performance feedback. Plans must specify desired outcomes in measurable terms. Furthermore, the people involved in the plans must frequently and frankly communicate about their progress in meeting performance objectives. Planning sets the standards against which performance will be measured and ultimately improved.

Planning begins a continuous loop of performance guidance and performance feedback. In the next chapter, we discuss the next function of management: organizing.

Chapter Five

Organizing Skills

AN OVERVIEW OF ORGANIZING

Organizing is the process of assigning people and allocating resources to accomplish the objectives set forth in the planning process. This means having qualified people and the resources they need in the right place at the right time so the action plan can succeed. During the planning process you decided what you are going to do; organizing is deciding how to do it.

Organizing is an ongoing concern. When planned objectives are not met, a manager may decide to reorganize. If the people taking inventory are showing up too early, before the current orders have been filled and before the new merchandise has been stocked, the manager has the power to find a different combination of people and resources that will be more productive. He or she may change the work flow, reassign workers to new supervisors, buy new equipment, or physically rearrange the workplace. He may change formal relationships, such as having the inventory people take direction from the stocking foreman, or promote informal relationships, such as having the leaders of the work groups assign "aisle captains" if he or she thinks this will increase efficiency. The manager may choose to solicit employee input before or after the reorganization takes place; he or she may choose to ask other departments or managers to participate. Organizing means figuring out how to make the action plan happen within the company's formal and informal organizations. Organizing skills are interpersonal communication skills and principles of supervision that optimize the resources of the organization.

UNDERSTANDING YOUR FORMAL ORGANIZATION

Take a blank piece of paper and write "ME" with a box around it in the center of the paper. List below this box everyone who reports directly to you and draw a line to them. Off to the side, list the people you interact with and draw solid or dotted lines to them. Finally, at the top of the page list names of those above you, continuing in this manner to represent as much of the rest of the organization as you know. This is a thumbnail sketch of your formal organization.

The formal organization prescribes formal relationships among people and resources. Presumably, these are organized in an optimal way that facilitates the accomplishment of the work of the organization. It is important for you to know how your company is organized, of course; it is just as important for you to understand why it's organized the way it is.

The dominant strategy of a company leads to its structure. A company creates a formal organization to maximize its human and other resources, and this formal organization depends in large part on what the company wants to accomplish.

The typical formal organization has a system of reporting, responsibility, and authority that reflects the formal power of the organization members. An informal system of interpersonal relationships, called the informal organization, springs up around the formal organization. For a company to work at its maximum effectiveness, the formal and informal organizations have to be supportive of each other.

You can be sure that your company's formal organization is generally suited to meet the needs of your business. Like most companies, yours probably evolved through different phases as it matured. Your company is organized and reorganized after periodic evaluations of the objectives of the business. The accomplishment of the company's objectives is the only good reason to organize in the first place, and it remains the only good reason to reorganize.

If a company is in a highly competitive industry, such as consumer electronics, for example, its organizational structure

FIGURE 5–1
An Organization's Strategy to Reach Its Objectives Dictates
Its Organizational Structure

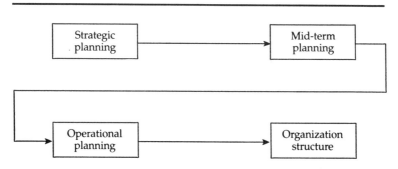

must provide certain types of communication and service at the point of sale. This type of company needs to be supported by a decentralized network of loyal and service-oriented retail dealers. The Federal Bureau of Investigation, on the other hand, has different organizational objectives that lead to a highly centralized system of information processing and autonomous field agents.

With its objectives in mind, the company must next decide what types of functions or work must be performed to accomplish those objectives. A manufacturer can organize around the major functions of production and marketing, for example.

Some functions are naturally associated with others, such as production and shipping, accounting and bookkeeping, engineering and research, production and quality control, and sales and marketing. If these functions can be grouped together, the organization will likely operate more efficiently because people who have to speak with each other frequently will be in close proximity. How functions are grouped will depend on the relative importance of the functions in a particular company. The process of grouping related functions or major work activities into manageable units is known as *departmentalization*.

You may be occasionally frustrated with the apparent illogic of your company's formal organization, but you can be confident that it is the way it is so that it can meet certain needs. Granted, the needs it is meeting may not be precisely current (which means the formal organization is lagging behind the company's development instead of leading it), but you are better off to accept it the way it is. Work within the structure you have for now—your energies are better spent on concerns where you can have a near-term positive impact.

When businesses develop their optimal organization, they usually find that parts of the company are centralized and other parts decentralized. A computer manufacturer, for example, may have a centralized manufacturing facility with a decentralized network of service providers spread throughout the country. Again, the structure reflects the organization's objectives.

Decentralization describes a physical relationship, but it also describes a management style. The degree of decentralization in a company can be quickly ascertained by asking one question: Which decisions are made by whom? If the local managers are allowed to make decisions involving large sums of money or affecting many employees, the organization is highly decentralized. On the other hand, if even the senior managers must check with headquarters to get approval on routine matters, the organization is highly centralized.

Regardless of the level of centralization a company selects, each position on the organizational chart has either a *line* or a *staff* relationship with the other positions.

Line positions are directly involved in doing the money-making work of the organization. They accomplish the primary purpose of the organization. Line positions constitute the core functions, processes, or departments that the company is organized around, such as the production department, the smelting division, or the marketing group.

Staff positions provide line departments with advice and assistance in specialized areas like personnel, finance, and research. The staff managers support the line managers and line workers at every level in the organization. The successful organization develops staff departments only to the size required to adequately service the needs of the line departments. Staff positions are auxiliary, described as either

(a) advisory, such as the legal department; (b) service, such as the research department, personnel department, or maintenance department; or (c) control, such as the accounting department or quality control department. Essentially, the formal organization serves the company's two types of customers: the line workers serve the "real" customers outside the company, while the staff workers serve the internal customers, who happen to be the line workers.

Realizing that the formal organization exists as it does for a reason may make it easier for you to work with it. The formal organization has been thoughtfully established to maximize the effective deployment of the company's resources. You can use the formal organization to your advantage to accomplish your goals. Ask your supervisor for a copy of the company's organizational chart. If there is no official organizational chart, piece one together yourself as you make your rounds to introduce yourself. At the very least, this will help you know with whom you should speak when you want to get something done.

UNDERSTANDING YOUR INFORMAL ORGANIZATION

Did you ever wonder why some people in your company always seem to be able to get things done with less effort? Did you ever wonder why some decisions languish in red tape and procedures, while other decisions are made quickly and efficiently? You are watching the informal organization in action.

The informal organization surrounds the formal organization. It is a complex and dynamic network of interpersonal relationships between organization members. These relationships cannot be diagrammed like the formal organization, yet they are just as important to the smooth operation of any group of people. By their nature, they are different for every company and are continually changing. Your success depends on your recognition and use of yours.

A company depends on its formal organization to provide a stable framework for starting and finishing work assignments. In the practical world, however, the members of the formal organization also modify the organization's structure to meet their own needs while carrying out the action plan, thereby creating an informal organization within and alongside the formal organization. Ideally, these organizations are mutually supportive and reinforce each other; when they are in conflict, the effectiveness of the company is crippled.

The informal organization is evident throughout the company in the form of informal or ad hoc work groups and friendships that cross functional lines. Customers may not be able to describe a company's informal organization, but they know it exists when they benefit from its spirit of cooperation and service. The informal organization has been described as the human side of the formal organization, and it is this intangible personality or corporate culture that distinguishes one enterprise from another.

The informal organization can never be completely controlled. Even if it were possible to do so, it might not be desirable. In the next few pages, we'll examine why the informal organization exists, how you can work with it, and its benefits and costs. In the process, you will gain a deeper understanding of organizational power and politics.

WHY DOES THE INFORMAL ORGANIZATION EXIST?

The informal organization is an inevitable byproduct of social interactions between people. To eliminate an informal organization would mean changing human nature or reducing the size of the organization to one person! In addition, there are at least three specific influences that support the continuation and regeneration of informal organizations.

First, the informal organization is a source of satisfaction for its members. We are a socially oriented people, and we want and need the companionship of peers. We are happiest when we are working among friends, and most of us value the sense that we belong to a network of friends at work. Surveys of worker attitudes reveal that one of the chief reasons for remaining with an employer, even in spite of unsatisfactory conditions or low advancement potential, is "because of the friends at work."

Second, the informal organization is a source of support for its members. The informal network helps its members solve problems, learn the organization's unwritten rules, overcome obstacles to success through personal coaching, sympathize with individual and group difficulties, and generally keep each other out of trouble. A person who cannot gain the support of his or her peer group is often unable to be effective.

Finally, the informal organization exists because it is a source of information for its members. Information is power in any organization, and most formal communication systems are inadequate in providing the news that is most important or interesting to the employees. Memos, newsletters, and bulletin-board postings are helpful, but they cannot compare with the company grapevine for the latest gossip and behind-the-scenes reporting. Employees depend on the informal organization for timely information about the positive and negative events in the company so they can prepare themselves for the results.

The informal communication channels provide more than just news; they are also important conduits for sharing experiences, fostering innovation and cooperation, generating support for new ideas, expressing consensus, collecting data for planning purposes, and directly or indirectly influencing people, groups, and events.

USING THE INFORMAL ORGANIZATION

Managers have mixed feelings about the informal organization, recognizing that it is very influential and yet generally beyond their control. The informal organization can add much to the quality of work life and overall productivity, but it also has the potential to sabotage the plans of managers.

Acknowledging the existence of the informal organization is the manager's first step toward understanding it. It is an inevitable, auxiliary structure that grows naturally out of human social processes. The manager cannot control it precisely, but he or she can create an environment that nurtures the informal organization in such a way that it contributes significantly to the realization of the organization's formal objectives.

A successful manager can attract the support of the informal organization. If he or she understands the informal network of power holders, he or she can focus on gaining the adjustments and accommodations desired from these people.

This conscious, directed use of the manager's power is commonly referred to as *organizational politics*, which is defined as interpersonal interactions that establish, acquire, transfer, and exercise power. The notion of politics carries an unfairly negative connotation. To the extent that we all want to be effective and gain the cooperation of those around us, we all need to participate in politics to some degree.

Finally, managing the informal organization requires an appreciation of its nature and its benefits. The manager must learn to live with the informal organization's vagueness ("Who started that rumor?"), its spirit ("You people surprise me with your attitude"), and the strength of its power ("In spite of everything I've tried, the team members persist in following the lead of someone else"). Like it or not, managers are a part of the informal organization by virtue of being members of the business. Successful managers learn to use their personal power to become active and effective participants in the informal organization.

THE STRUCTURE OF THE INFORMAL ORGANIZATION

The informal organization is not without structure. Like the formal organization, the informal organization is based on the relative power an individual holds, but it encompasses a broader base of personal power in addition to the power associated with a formal position of authority.

Power is a complex concept, but for our purposes, we can define it simply as the ability of one person to influence the behavior of another. Power is neither good nor bad but simply an inevitable aspect of every human association, formal or informal. The power structure of a company's informal organization, which essentially links people together on an interpersonal level, is too complex to depict with a two-dimensional organizational chart. How the informal organization works, however, can be understood by examining the different types of personal power.

There are five types of personal power, most of which are not under the control of management.

Positional power. When a person is in a position of formal authority, he or she has positional power. Group members believe a person with formal authority ought to have influence over them because of the unique responsibilities associated with the formal position. Most people believe it is their duty to obey a police officer or a vice president because of the formal authority these two positions carry, even though most people are not directly accountable to these positions. Because of their positions, it is assumed that those with formal authority "know what is right."

Reward power. Reward power is derived from a person's ability to reward another individual. Some reward powers are formal, such as when a manager rewards a person with a promotion or an increase in compensation. Informal reward powers are exercised by co-workers and informal leaders in the form of acceptance or rejection by co-workers, recognition for performance, certain types of assistance, and the sharing or withholding of information.

Referent power. This form of power is evident when group members identify with the power holder. If they like the power holder and want to be like him, they will do what the power holder asks out of a sense of respect, liking, and desire to be liked in return. President John F. Kennedy had strong referent power, his admonition, "Ask not what your country can do for you, but what you can do for your country," became a rallying cry for a generation of Americans committed to social action through organizations like the Peace Corps.

Coercive power. Coercive power is the power to punish or remove rewards. In the informal organization, this can take the form of avoidance, withdrawal of friendship, or exclusion from group activities or discussion. When exercised by several group members at once, this type of punishment by peers can be very powerful. No one likes to be punished, however, so using this type of power can be counterproductive in the long run.

Expert power. This very effective form of power is based on a person's special knowledge or skill. When other group members recognize a person's unique ability to contribute to their collective success, they naturally defer to him or her.

Experts can be troublesome to manage. If a computer programmer, for example, becomes so knowledgeable about a computer system as to be indispensable, the manager with the formal authority may be reluctant to discipline him for fear that the programmer will quit or sabotage the system.

This highlights the inherent conflict between line and staff positions. The line position has the formal authority and legitimate power, while the staff positions depend on informal, expert power. The line manager may have the authority to manage, but in practice, his power is shared among the experts in the informal organization. Imagine what happens at a staff meeting when the line manager says, "We're going to handle that problem by doing such and such," and one or more experts in the group says, "That's wrong, it's a bad idea." The most successful line managers have at least one area of expertise and are prudent enough to ask for the advice of the experts in other matters.

Five Types of Personal Power

Positional	sounds like this:	"Do this because I'm the boss."
Reward	sounds like this:	"Do this and I will make it worth your effort."
Referent	sounds like this:	"Do as I do."
Coercive	sounds like this:	"Do this or else."
Expert	sounds like this:	"Do this because I know what to do and you don't."

THE BENEFITS OF THE INFORMAL ORGANIZATION

Once managers accept the inevitability of the informal organization, they can begin to focus on its benefits and strive to create the environment to foster its significant contributions. The chief benefits are listed in the following paragraphs.

To help communication. The company grapevine is the informal communication network that coexists with the formal or official channels of communication. The informal organization can transmit information throughout a company faster than the official channels with a degree of accuracy that can be astonishing. Informal communications can be highly selective and very responsive, too. The official channels of communication—memos, meetings, newsletters, etc.—are still needed to provide complete and credible information, but the grapevine is a valuable contribution of the informal organization.

To help get tasks accomplished. Managers do not always acknowledge when they use the informal organization, but they invariably rely upon it to get work done. When subordinates are granted the flexibility to cross the official lines of the formal organization chart in order to solve problems, they are using the informal organization. Imagine how ponderous and inefficient an organization would be if all requests for action and information had to be channeled through one or more supervisors. The informal organization provides an effective framework for problem solving that makes good use of the subordinates' interpersonal skills and capitalizes on their natural desire to do their job well.

To increase worker satisfaction. Because of the informal organization, employees are more satisfied with their jobs. They are more confident their contributions are recognized and appreciated, they are more secure about their jobs because they know what is going on in the company, and they are more committed and loyal because they care about their relationships with their co-workers. These intangible features of the informal organization translate into tangible benefits for the organization, such as lower turnover rates, lower recruitment expenses, less absenteeism, a better safety record, and even higher job performance. The informal organization is the extension of our natural desire to build satisfying relationships with our co-workers.

To complement the formal organization. The informal organization augments the formal organization in several important ways. First, it provides temporary assistance to those who need on-the-job training. Virtually everyone needs to talk through a problem or situation at some time, and there are no boxes for informal advisors or mentors on the formal organization chart. Without an informal support network, people would be trying to perform without feedback or advice, isolated and alienated.

Also, managers find they can supervise more people when they have the support of an active informal organization. By trusting subordinates to interact with each other regularly, a manager needs to spend less time micromanaging every action of every employee. Managers who are genuinely interested in achieving the organization's objectives through the efforts of others will not pass up the opportunity to use the resources and power of the informal organization.

Finally, the informal organization complements the formal organization by challenging and encouraging better management. An informal organization that draws the best efforts out of subordinates will draw the best efforts from the managers, too. Managers should realize that worker cooperation and enthusiasm affect the organization's performance; not wanting to lose this positive momentum generated by the informal organization, the manager will work hard to make the most of his or her opportunities. If the manager and subordinates are mutually supportive, yet challenging each other to be the best they can be, they both benefit from a more successful organization.

THE COSTS OF THE
INFORMAL ORGANIZATION

The informal organization is not without shortcomings. Because it cannot be controlled, it can disrupt routines, undermine management's directives, depress morale, sabotage operations, and discourage innovation.

Operationally, the informal organization can make or break a company. If the leaders of the informal organization decide to rebel or thwart the wishes of management, the formal organization can do very little before it happens. With sufficient peer pressure, the informal organization's leadership may be able to slow down and otherwise disrupt the efficient operation of the business by persuading other employees to stop doing their jobs as well as they can. Fortunately, most people realize that permanently crippling the company will hurt each employee in the long run. Widespread and malicious actions rarely continue for very long, giving way to discussions and negotiations between the factions who disagree. This is a negative effect of the informal organization using its power, but it can have a positive outcome if communication within the organization improves.

A more insidious cost of the informal organization is lowered productivity caused by role conflict, conformity, and resistance to change. The personal influence an informal leader has with an employee may conflict with the manager who holds positional power. The resulting confusion will almost certainly slow down the work of the employee. At best, the employee will struggle to satisfy the wishes of two bosses; at worst, he or she will be forced to sacrifice his or her work record in the tug-of-war between the manager and informal leader.

The "group think" promoted by the informal organization can lead to a numbing conformity. In organizations with strong informal networks, individual differences, personal expression, and personal ambition may be discouraged. "We don't do things like that here," and "You're making the rest of us look bad," and, "You have to try harder to fit in," are some of the comments a worker may hear from the informal leaders. Petty jealousies and competition may also result in a common level of mediocre performance.

For the same reasons, new ideas and innovation are not always welcome. "We've always done it this way. If it isn't broken, don't fix it," is a typical remark indicating a reluctance to try new ideas. This attitude can stop new ideas before they have a chance to work.

In the next chapter, we discuss the third management function: influence.

Chapter Six

Influencing Skills

Business folklore is rich with stories about companies achieving extraordinary success with ordinary employees. When asked how theirs became such high performance organizations, the firms' presidents modestly say, "We're lucky. We have good people."

In fact, luck has little to do with good performance on the job. More likely, these companies have good managers who can motivate and lead others. By directing the efforts of others, the managers see to it that the organizations' objectives are accomplished. Influencing is the third function of management.

THE MANAGER IS AN INFLUENCER

The manager is responsible for making the organization get things done. As we learned in earlier chapters, he or she begins by planning what the organization is going to do and then organizes the resources required to get the work done. After planning and organizing, the manager is logically the person best prepared to supervise the implementation of the plans—*if* he or she can persuade others to help.

Inevitably, managing means completing tasks through the efforts of other people. Assembling lamps, producing a new product, erecting a building—no matter what the task, the manager cannot succeed alone. To see his or her plans implemented, the manager must influence the actions or behaviors of others and direct their efforts.

Managers influence people by motivating them and leading them. Motivation and leadership are interpersonal skills that communicate the relationship between all employee's needs and the organization's objectives. By motivating and leading, the manager can build a task-oriented team, a cohesive and efficient work unit, thereby amplifying the productivity of the group.

Motivation is defined as the willingness to put forth effort in the pursuit of organizational goals. It is a level of activity, a behavior that can be observed. It is not the same as job performance; a person can be highly motivated to program computers and still be evaluated as incompetent. Motivation is as complex as human nature, and every person's reasons for working are likely to be slightly different. Nevertheless, if a manager has a basic understanding of motivation theory, he or she will be better prepared to influence employee efforts and thereby improve performance.

Leadership is that combination of personal characteristics that earn a person the privilege of significantly influencing a group or individual. Not all leaders are managers, but every manager must be a leader. Leadership is the role performed by the person who speaks up and persuasively communicates the organizational objectives, thus energizing the motivation process.

Understanding motivation will help the manager know what to say; understanding leadership will help the manager know how to say it. There is no one best way to motivate or lead people; however, there are basic guidelines and principles, and these will be the focus of this chapter.

GETTING RESULTS THROUGH MOTIVATION

The challenge of all managers is to effectively motivate their workers to work toward the organization's objectives. The more we understand about motivation, the more likely we will be able to effectively influence or direct the behavior of employees. Thanks to much study by social scientists, contemporary management recognizes that motivation is a complicated process. Important aspects to keep in mind when discussing motivation include the following:

Motivation is a set of psychological processes that energize voluntary behavior. Most motivation theories suggest that the psychological processes are stimulated or triggered by internal needs that are aroused. However, there is still much discussion and study that seek to pinpoint those exact needs.

Motivation is action directed toward specific goals intended to satisfy needs. These goals are not necessarily the most desirable or appropriate goals from the manager's viewpoint, but they are voluntarily chosen by a person because they will satisfy a need.

Motivation is not the same as performance. It is a description of behaviors, such as working quickly to stock shelves or making a certain number of sales calls. The fact that an employee is motivated, of course, does not mean that he or she is stocking the shelves correctly or closing sales.

Your challenge is to motivate your employees to do their best work. By understanding some of the basic theories of motivation, you will be better prepared to find the successful combination that inspires improved performance in your employees. Again, you need to find ways to align your employees' interests with the interests of the company. This challenge is depicted in Figure 6–1.

No management approach is applicable to all situations; likewise, theories of motivation each have distinct differences. In this section, we will examine three of the major theories about work motivation that are the roots of many contemporary management techniques: the needs theory, the motivation-hygiene theory, and the expectancy theory. We will then look at how these theories can be applied to influence employee motivation. Don't be overwhelmed by these theories— they are simply different ways of thinking about why employees do what they do, and any additional thinking we can do about this topic will be useful.

FIGURE 6–1
*Managers Must Align Employees' Personal Goals and Needs
with Those of the Company*

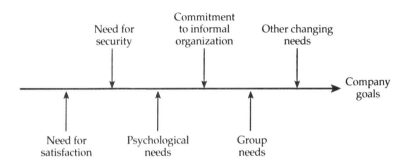

Needs Theories

Abraham Maslow, one of the pioneer behavioral scientists, introduced his hierarchy-of-needs theory in 1943. According to Maslow's theory, people are motivated by needs they want to satisfy. He grouped needs into five distinct types: physiological, safety, social, esteem (recognition and status), and self-fulfillment (realization of one's unique and complete potential) needs. These needs are hierarchical, or arranged in the sequence in which they must be satisfied.

Maslow's theory of human motivation is based on the following assumptions:

- Needs that are not satisfied motivate or influence behavior.
- As long as needs are unsatisfied, they monopolize a person's consciousness and have virtually exclusive power to motivate behavior.
- As soon as needs are satisfied, they lose the power to motivate.
- Needs are satisfied according to a hierarchy of importance. The lowest level of unmet need must be sufficiently satisfied before the next level of need becomes important enough to have the power to motivate.

Social scientist David McClelland suggests that the needs which determine behavior are secondary needs that augment Maslow's universal needs. His needs theory is concerned with how individual needs and environmental factors combine to form three basic motives: the need for achievement, the need for power, and the need for affiliation. According to this theory, each of these three motives evokes a different sense of satisfaction. Every individual has each of these motives in varying degrees, but one motive will be dominant in most situations and will determine most of a person's behavior.

McClelland maintains that because these motives explain most behavior, employees can be categorized and motivated accordingly. The probability that an individual will perform a job effectively depends upon a combination of the strength of the motive or need relative to other needs, the possibility of success in performing the task, and the strength value of the incentive or reward for performance.

Managers find it useful in recruitment and selection of personnel to understand that certain jobs are best performed by people predisposed to a particular motivation. For example, to the extent that a job requires calculated risk-taking and rigorous goal-setting behavior, an achievement-motivated person will do better than a power-oriented or affiliation-oriented person. Likewise, if the successful performance of a job requires cooperation, an affiliation-motivated person will do the best job. If the job requires influencing others, and all other factors are equal, a power-oriented person will be most successful.

Motivation-Hygiene Theory

Another motivation theory that many managers have found useful is Fredrick Herzberg's motivation-hygiene theory. Herzberg found that the aspects of people's jobs that made them feel good or satisfied were factors intrinsic to the job itself. These factors included achievement, recognition, the work itself, responsibility, advancement, and personal growth. Herzberg called these sources of satisfaction *motivators*, since they apparently were necessary for substantial improvements in work performance.

Herzberg also found that when people described why and when they were dissatisfied with their jobs, many talked about conditions surrounding their jobs rather than the job itself. Some of the factors mentioned were company policy and administration, their relationship with their supervisor, work conditions, salary, relationships with peers, relationships with subordinates, personal problems, status, and security. Herzberg called these sources of dissatisfaction *hygiene* or *maintenance factors* because they comprise the work environment rather than the work itself.

According to Herzberg, satisfaction and dissatisfaction are not opposite ends of the same continuum; rather, they are entirely separate dimensions that must be dealt with in different ways. Satisfaction is affected by motivators—those factors relating to the job content, and dissatisfaction is affected by hygiene or maintenance factors—those factors relating to the job environment. Note that removing negative hygiene factors does not automatically heighten motivation. It does, however, clear the way for one or more motivators to have a positive effect.

Herzberg is generally credited with the concept of job enrichment as a motivator. This concept, in turn, has contributed to the notion of worker empowerment. Empowerment is a compelling motivator by itself. It is a proven approach to facilitating performance improvement that we'll look at in detail in Chapter 7.

Expectancy Theory

The needs theories do not adequately account for differences in individual employees or explain why people behave in certain ways. The *expectancy-instrumentality-valence theory* is based on what the employee believes about his behavior and what he perceives as important or of value. The key concepts of the expectancy theory are that motivation depends on:

- The belief that a person's effort will result in performance; this is referred to as *expectancy*.
- The belief that a person's performance will be rewarded; this is referred to as *instrumentality*.
- The perceived value an individual places on a specific outcome; this is referred to as *valence*.

According to the expectancy theory, all of these factors—expectancy, instrumentality, and valence of rewards—must be present before a high level of motivation can occur.

The manager's goal should be to provide outcomes that subordinates highly value and to ensure that they perceive a high probability of those outcomes occurring if they behave as desired.

Expectancy: The "Thinking" Side of Motivation

"I believe that if I do this . . .	. . . it will lead to that . . .	. . . and then cause this to occur,	therefore I will act in this manner."

A Final Theory: The Contingency Approach

The optimistic aspect of contemporary management is that there are no built-in reasons why work cannot be pleasant and satisfying, or why employees' constructive work behavior cannot be encouraged. However, the unpredictability of employee responses to the work environment suggests that a combination of motivational theories may be most effective in a specific situation or at a particular work site. A healthy measure of common sense and practical experience drawn from that which has yielded positive results in the past should also be added. This results-oriented approach is commonly referred to as the *contingency approach*.

The contingency approach acknowledges that there is no single best management philosophy that is equally accurate or effective in all circumstances. There are no plans, organizational structures, influencing techniques or controls that will fit all situations. Instead, managers must find unique ways to be effective in each situation.

The contingency approach urges avoidance of any unthinking, wholesale application of a single philosophy. Instead, the manager should engage in healthy experimentation within the guidelines of the main theories, and embrace the pragmatic solutions that work better than others. Motivating employees means identifying those needs that will cause employees to act, and then clearly communicating the probability that those needs will be satisfied when employees contribute their efforts toward accomplishing organizational tasks.

GETTING RESULTS THROUGH LEADERSHIP

An understanding of motivation theory does not automatically translate into motivated employees. Once the needs of the employees have been identified, or the motivators have been selected, someone has to speak up and communicate the organizational objectives. You, as a company leader, are that person—you have to make something happen by exercising influencing skills in your position as a leader.

Leadership causes others to do what the leader wants them to do. A good leader is one who motivates others to put forth their best efforts. Leaders can come by their leadership skills intuitively, but leadership can also be learned. Lee Iacocca, the leader of the Chrysler recovery in the early 1980s, certainly demonstrated the ability to inspire others and draw extraordinary performance from them. But like other strong leaders, Iacocca's skills went beyond charisma. He learned what motivates individual workers and used this knowledge to direct their activities.

The Power of the Leader

Every group has a leader, and that person's leadership begins with power. A leader's source of power logically reinforces his or her position of greatest influence; after all, the leaders of groups usually control the distribution of resources, rewards, and punishments. Leaders also control the duties and assignments made to specific people, and they often select basic group goals. Given this authority, it is not surprising that other group members orient themselves toward and readily accept influence from leaders.

A leader's power will come from one or both of two sources: traditional power sources that depend on the person's position within the organization, or personal power sources that are based on personal characteristics recognized by group members.

Traditional or positional power attributed to a leader is signaled by a specific position or title. This source of power stays with the position—whoever carries that title has the power that goes with it. It is typically oriented downward on the organizational chart, can be delegated, and works best with tasks that do not require specific individuals to complete them.

Personal power is much more likely to be associated with a natural or intuitive leader who may lack an official position, but nevertheless earns an informal position of influence. Personal power travels with a person because it arises from personal characteristics. If an individual with personal power moves to a new position or joins a new committee, he or she will influence the groups involved almost immediately. Personal power is oriented upward on the organizational chart and works equally well with tasks and people. Personal power is generally regarded as stronger than positional power, and when the two clash, personal power usually wins.

Power is limited by the type or types of power that the leader has. We first discussed power in Chapter 5 in the context of the informal organization. A leader can have more than one of the following five bases of power, but they must be acquired in the order presented to avoid the abuse of power or a lack of credibility.

Positional power. Group members believe that a leader with a defined position above them in the organization power ought to have power over them. A manager newly transferred, for example, is still a manager. The new manager starts the first day on the new job with the power incumbent with his or her position.

Referent power. Group members identify with or want to be like a leader with referent power and therefore comply out of a sense of respect, liking, and wanting to be liked. These leaders are often described as charismatic.

Reward power. A leader has reward power over group members if he or she has the ability to deliver positive consequences (such as letting people leave work early) or remove negative consequences (such as improving working conditions) in response to their behavior.

Coercive power. A leader has coercive power over other group members if he or she can mete out negative consequences (such as reprimands, demotions, or extra work assignments) or remove positive consequences (such as blocking promotions) in response to the behavior of group members.

Expert power. Managers have expert power to the extent that subordinates or others attribute knowledge and expertise to them. If you are regarded as a subject-matter expert only, you are limited to leadership in only well-defined areas, such as engineering or the personnel department, but not both.

Leadership is not management. A good manager is a good leader, but a good leader is not necessarily a successful manager. Managers are generally associated with administrative, technical, and verbal skills, while leaders have strong interpersonal, coaching, counseling, and advocacy skills. Leaders also are acknowledged agents of change within an organization because they have sufficient personal power to introduce new ideas and persuade others to try them. Effective leaders understand their base and sources of power and use leadership styles appropriate to the situation, to their followers, and to their relative position within the group.

Leadership Styles

Because leaders are highly visible within every organization, they have received more than their fair share of scrutiny and study. Researchers and management theorists generally agree that there are four basic leadership styles:

1. *Autocratic leaders* tell subordinates what to do and expect to be obeyed without question. Autocratic leaders assume they will have to coerce, control, or threaten employees to motivate them. Their strength is their decisiveness; their weakness is their failure to inspire subordinates to do their best work.

2. *Participative leaders* involve subordinates in decisions but retain final authority. They share a strong mutual respect with their subordinates for each other's technical expertise and input. Participative leaders assume that employees desire greater responsibility in the organization. This style enhances job satisfaction but slows the decision-making process.

3. *Democratic leaders* try to do what the majority of subordinates desire. They value consensus above efficiency, and rely on rationality and thorough explanations to influence the group.

4. *Laissez-faire leaders* are uninvolved with the work of the group. This appears to work only with groups that are highly expert and well motivated so that the need for leadership is minimized, such as with groups of scientists.

Because of the manager's position in the organization, his or her leadership style will do much to establish the attitudes and work habits of the group. There are exceptions, of course, but the employees usually reflect the manager's style. The manager's assumptions about employees and his or her relationship with them has a profound effect on the management policies, communication patterns, and quality of work environment in the organization.

Assumptions about how others will behave actually affects how they do behave. This is called the concept of *self-fulfilling prophecy*, and is summarized in four principles:

1. Managers (and everyone else, too) hold certain assumptions and expectations of people or events.

Comparing Leadership Styles: Advantages and Disadvantages

	Advantages	Disadvantages
Autocratic	Improves productivity Helpful in high-pressure situations Speeds decision-making process	Does not make the most of employees' ideas or skills Reduces employee job satisfaction
Participative	Raises employee job satisfaction Fosters strong commitment to the organization Preferred by most employees	Slow decision-making process Raises doubts about the leader's competence and/or strength
Democratic	Value placed on reaching consensus ensures complete discussion of decisions The best idea usually wins	Least efficient Begs the question, "Whose decision is this?" Group process can be manipulative
Laissez-faire	Expects and recognizes competence and motivation of employees Nurtures individual contributions and creativity	Unsettling for people who want or need structure Possible deficiencies in communication within and between work groups

2. These assumptions and expectations are communicated to others via various cues.

3. People tend to respond to these cues by adjusting their behavior to match them.

4. The result is that the original expectation becomes true, thus reinforcing the original expectation and creating a cycle of self-fulfilling prophecies.

The following theories will provide a framework for discussing leadership style and its impact on the productivity of the organization.

Theory X and Theory Y

Two opposing philosophies of human nature at work have been distinguished by management theorist Douglas McGregor. Traditional management assumptions about workers have been grouped loosely together and comprise *Theory X.* More positive and optimistic philosophies about employees are called *Theory Y.*

The Theory X philosophy of management assumes that workers are by nature selfish, lazy, lacking in ambition, reluctant to assume responsibility, and indifferent to organizational needs. In other words, the Theory X approach presumes that most or all workers are by nature unmotivated to work.

If a manager subscribes to this pessimistic philosophy, his management techniques are likely to reflect his distrust of worker's motives and his generally low expectations for worker performance. This suggests that the Theory X manager must coerce, control, or threaten employees in order to motivate them. This philosophy has prevailed for centuries and is still very common today.

The more optimistic philosophy of human nature at work is called Theory Y. This is often referred to as the human relations approach to management. Supporters of Theory Y assume that workers are not passive participants in the organization's development but rather desire increasing amounts of responsibility and skill development in accordance with the organization's needs.

The Theory Y philosophy makes some assumptions about management, too. The human relations approach depends on supportive management practices that enable workers to develop their own potential. It also depends on the workers to bring a team-oriented attitude to their jobs.

Theory X and Theory Y Offer Alternate Assumptions about Employees

Theory X	Theory Y
Most people dislike work; work only because they believe the have to, and avoid it if possible	Most people want to do good work and be recognized for it
	Work is as natural as play or rest
Most people lack responsibility	Most people want to be well managed
Most people lack ambition	
Most people seek security above all else	Most people exercise self-direction and self-control in the service of objectives to which they are committed
Most people must be coerced, controlled, and threatened with punishment before they get to work	
	Most people have potential
With these assumptions, Theory X managers seek results by coercing and controlling employees	Most people seek and accept responsibility under the proper conditions; they have imagination, ingenuity, and creativity that can be applied to work
	With these assumptions, Theory Y managers seek results by creating work environments that develop the potential of employees

Theory X and Theory Y are neither good nor bad; they are simply effective or ineffective in specific situations. The following theories offer similarly useful frameworks that help the manager think about leadership.

The Leadership Grid®

The Leadership Grid has gained wide acceptance as a useful diagnostic tool for ailing management systems that need to see themselves from an entirely new perspective. The Leadership Grid is a two-dimensional matrix that relates a manager's concern for people (vertical axis) with concern for production or task completion (horizontal axis). The grid is 9×9; the higher the number, the higher the level of concern. Through a series of questions, the leadership style can be plotted and visually portrayed.

The Leadership Grid depicts five major leadership styles:

- (1,1) Impoverished Management: The manager has little concern for either people or production.

- (9,1) Authority Compliance Management: The manager stresses efficient operation through controls; he or she tries to minimize situations where people can interfere. This manager wants production at any cost.

- (5,5) Middle of the Road Management: The manager attempts to balance and trade off concern for tasks in exchange for a satisfactory level of morale. This manager is a compromiser.

- (1,9) Country Club Management: The manager is thoughtful, comfortable, and friendly, and very likely to try for consensus. This manager has little concern for output.

- (9,9) Team Management: The manager seeks high output through committed people; he or she has high expectations in terms of mutual trust, respect, and interdependence.

Since the Leadership Grid was introduced in the early 1960s (it was formerly called the Managerial Grid), it has been suggested that the 9,9 team management position is the most effective. The reasons are self evident: a high concern for output or people that does not compromise the other axis will yield highly satisfied employees who are highly productive. The grid is a way to visualize the current and desired position of the leadership team. At the very least, it raises the expectations the manager sets for himself, thereby laying the groundwork for a new self-fulfilling prophecy.

The Leadership Continuum

Since the leadership continuum is the graphic representation of the exchanges that occur between a manager's use of authority and the freedom that subordinates experience

FIGURE 6–2

The Manager Must Balance Concern for People with Concern for Production

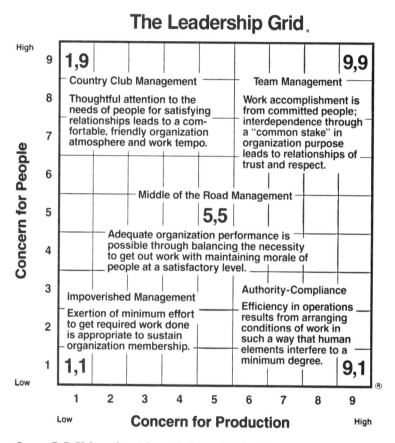

The Leadership Grid ®

Concern for People (vertical axis, Low to High, 1–9)
Concern for Production (horizontal axis, Low to High, 1–9)

1,9 Country Club Management
Thoughtful attention to the needs of people for satisfying relationships leads to a comfortable, friendly organization atmosphere and work tempo.

9,9 Team Management
Work accomplishment is from committed people; interdependence through a "common stake" in organization purpose leads to relationships of trust and respect.

5,5 Middle of the Road Management
Adequate organization performance is possible through balancing the necessity to get out work with maintaining morale of people at a satisfactory level.

1,1 Impoverished Management
Exertion of minimum effort to get required work done is appropriate to sustain organization membership.

9,1 Authority-Compliance
Efficiency in operations results from arranging conditions of work in such a way that human elements interfere to a minimum degree.

Source: R. R. Blake and A. Adams McCanse. "The Leadership Grid Figure for Leadership Dilemmas—Grid Solutions," (Houston: Gulf Publishing Company). Copyright 1991 by Scientific Methods, Inc. Reproduced by permission of the owners.

as leadership styles shift from boss-centered to employee-centered. The model was developed by Robert Tannenbaum and Warren H. Schmidt and depicts a series of factors that influence a manager's selection of the most appropriate leadership style.

Here is how the leadership continuum model works. As the manager gives up authority, the subordinate accepts additional freedom. For example, a manager may use a more participative leadership style when subordinates:

- Seek independence.
- Understand and are committed to the goals of the organization.
- Are well educated and experienced in performing the job.
- Seek responsibility for decision making.
- Expect a participative style of leadership.

When the above conditions do not exist, the manager may need to adopt a more autocratic leadership style. The most effective managers will be neither task-centered nor people-centered, but rather flexible enough to respond to different situations with a variable style that shares as much authority with the employee as the employee is prepared to accept.

Which Leadership Style Is Best?

Given that many approaches to leadership are learned in the process of becoming an effective manager, the desire for a single best leadership style is understandable. However, as we have already seen in other areas of management, there is no single best answer.

Most of the theorists agree that a model must accommodate the differences between situations and the differences between leaders in order to be useful. Factors affecting the choice of leadership style include the manager's philosophy of human nature, experiences, training, and professional and technical competence. Similarly, the workers' belief systems, attitudes toward work and authority, maturity levels, experience, and skill levels will determine the leadership style that is most effective.

Imagine how these additional factors will affect a manager's leadership style:

- The number of people in the work group.
- The types of tasks.
- Situational stress.
- Objectives of the unit.
- The presence or absence of a union.
- The leadership style of the manager's boss.
- The overall relationship of the manager with the subordinates.

THE PAYOFF: INCREASED PRODUCTIVITY

It is hard work to motivate and lead employees. Not only does it require considerable skill development on the part of the manager, but it may also be exhausting. Remember that the manager is working in a fluid social environment inside the organization, an environment that can never be fully controlled. By the nature of the job, he or she has to be prepared to respond to many eventualities, shifting his or her leadership style in the process.

Is it worth it? On a personal level, most managers probably feel that it is. Their needs for recognition and self-fulfillment are partially met by being effective in their job, and they have the satisfaction of seeing their plans and visions for the organization amplified through the efforts of others.

Improved productivity for the organization is the greatest benefit. A skilled manager who can motivate and lead others can dramatically improve the output of an organization, without increasing costs, simply by maximizing the human resources.

Companies are increasingly putting management theories into practice, with profitable results. Volvo has put new motivation and leadership ideas to work on a large scale at their auto plant in Kalmar, Sweden. A new managing director interpreted the 41 percent annual turnover rate, in spite of high salaries, to mean that the workers did not like their jobs. Indeed, upon closer inspection, he learned that highly educated employees were being asked to perform increasingly monotonous, tedious jobs. They didn't feel good about themselves, and they were frustrated with the company. The manager suspected that many quality problems stemmed from the poor performance caused by these negative feelings.

By adopting a highly participative leadership style, he involved key employee leaders in the plant's productivity and quality problems. Though doubtful at first that their suggestions would be taken seriously, the employees soon became committed to redesigning the assembly line as a solution to both problems.

The result was a new plant with a lot of new ideas and fresh enthusiasm. The old assembly line with one person doing one task all day was replaced by 25 work teams consisting of 15 to 25 workers. Each team was responsible for one aspect of production, such as the electrical system. As long as the team met the production quota, they could organize themselves in any way they liked. Job rotation became commonplace. Coupled with other employee-centered design features like windows, music, and quieter work environments, turnover plummeted, training costs dropped, productivity began to rise, and quality ceased to be a problem. Why? Because the employees were treated with respect and given an opportunity to participate in decisions that affected their work place. While the plant was not a democracy, it was a far cry from the product-centered management style of the manager's predecessor. The production requirements stayed the same, but the workers could decide how the job was to get done. Would a similar version of employee empowerment work in your company, too?

As more firms develop new ways to motivate and lead their employees, they enjoy higher productivity. The lesson for the new manager is clear: your efforts to invent ever-better ways to influence your workers will pay generous dividends.

Chapter Seven

Facilitating Skills

Facilitating is the fourth and final management function in our performance improvement model. It follows planning, organizing, and influencing, then leads directly back to planning, thereby starting the process of improving performance all over again. The facilitating function reconciles the differences between actual performance and expected performance with the help of empowered workers.

This is a long overdue evolution in management thinking. It has profound implications for how you manage your people, how you solve problems, and how you achieve results.

Traditionally, this final step in the performance improvement model has been called "control." The portrayal of the manager as the controller of performance, in effect, casts the manager in the role of performance policeman, which often seems to promote a negative relationship between manager and worker. It implies, "As a manager, I'll do my best to plan, organize, and influence to get the performance I want; but if it doesn't happen, I'll step in with rewards and punishments that manipulate workers into better performance."

The notion of manager-as-controller is now generally regarded as a narrow, outdated view. It suggests the manager can somehow correct performance deficiencies by himself, without the cooperation or collaboration of his employees. The contemporary manager is more likely to be a facilitator of performance, working side-by-side with like-minded workers who share the same performance goals.

The evolution of this function from control to facilitation marks an important shift and expansion in our understanding of what it means to be a manager. Reconciling actual and expected performance, which is the essence of this function, is no longer as simple as catching your employees doing something wrong (or right) so you can apply the appropriate negative (or positive) reinforcement. Several dominant trends in the workplace—such as more work being done by groups, both formally and informally, and workers' rising expectations for participation—reward the facilitating manager and punish the controlling manager.

THE MANAGER AS A FACILITATOR

Facilitate is a psychological term that means to make performance easier by lessening resistance. Most of us know this term already in the context of interpersonal communications. Facilitating small group discussions, for example, means clarifying agendas, soliciting input from those who are saying too little, reining in those who are saying too much, and generally managing the conversation by removing the obstacles to clear, conclusive communication.

When applied to management, facilitate literally means to improve performance by removing the obstacles that stand in the way of improved performance. Putting it another way, the manager facilitates performance improvement by removing obstacles to greater productivity. Such obstacles include resistance to change, inadequate equipment, inefficient procedures, lack of good communication, lack of focus and/or accountability relative to tasks, insufficient training resources, and so on.

Think about it this way: improving performance means aligning actual performance with the performance we expected or predicted when we wrote our original work plans (remember the planning function?). Somehow, we have to reconcile the gap between these two levels of performance. Determining the difference between actual and expected performance is relatively easy if the work plan includes performance standards and measurements.

FIGURE 7–1
Performance Gaps Are the Difference Between Actual and Expected Performance

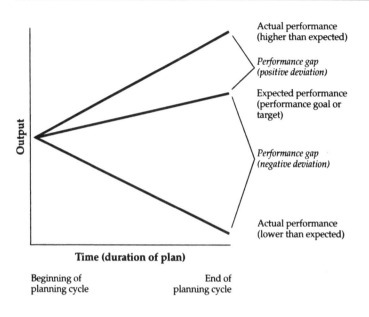

Actual performance (higher than expected)

Performance gap (positive deviation)

Expected performance (performance goal or target)

Performance gap (negative deviation)

Actual performance (lower than expected)

Output

Time (duration of plan)

Beginning of planning cycle

End of planning cycle

Therefore, as a facilitating manager, you will review the planner performance (the performance expectations); evaluate the actual performance of the workers to determine whether there is a positive or negative deviation from the expected performance (the performance gap); and close performance gaps by reconciling the difference between actual and expected performance.

The facilitating function is the time the manager steps back, takes a wide-angle snapshot of what has been accomplished during a period of time, and asks: How are we doing? If we aren't doing as well as we want to be, why not? How can we improve our performance? If we are doing better than we expected, what should be our new performance goal? In short, facilitating begins with a look at the performance standards of one plan, and ends with the updated performance standards of the next plan. Somehow, the manager has to get from one to the other.

What's the best way to bridge the performance gap?

In a word, empowerment. Empowered workers are those who share in the decision-making process. By sharing the authority and responsibility for reconciling performance gaps, the manager is most likely to see steady performance improvement.

Facilitating Performance Improvement Means Managing Empowered Workers

Updating performance expectations, and changing the quality and/or quantity of work performed by the workers who are going to accomplish those new expectations, can be tricky. To do it, you will need the help of an empowered workforce. Only when workers are empowered are they truly committed to positive changes in performance levels. Only when workers are empowered are they motivated to take the initiative to make decisions, solve problems, monitor their progress, and thereby direct their own work plans.

Empowerment is defined as the belief and corresponding behavior that one has some power—meaning autonomy, authority, or control—over significant aspects of one's life.

Empowerment is a value, not a program or set of procedures. It is a concept of working together, an approach to solving problems together, in order to reconcile performance gaps. It is built into the dynamic culture of your company in a unique way that works for you. It is more than participative management, which just asks for people's help, because empowerment gets people to help themselves.

Consider the following story: A printer with about 90 employees hired a new plant manager. The printer, who was the entrepreneur who started the business, had finally admitted he could no longer run the entire production schedule out of his shirt pocket. He handed the new manager the keys and told him to "fix whatever is wrong" so the company could begin earning the profits it was supposedly capable of earning.

The new manager had been a vice president of finance at another printer, so he knew the printing business, but he had never managed this many people before. He was shocked when he looked at the overall plant performance. He studied what types of jobs the plant did well, and what types of jobs the plant did not-so-well. Every other job, it seemed, was an expensive, money-losing crisis requiring overtime, extra stock for redos, extra shipping for overnight delivery, and other financially draining measures.

Being a politically-correct kind of guy, he held a series of meetings with the employees. What's going on here? he asked. Why are these types of jobs chronic losers?

Warily, the employees offered their opinions:

"We never say no to a job, no matter how unrealistic the customer's deadline."

"The sales people make promises for delivery without checking the production schedule first. Then, they come back into the shop and shamelessly beg for us to somehow get it done."

"The pressmen have excuses, but no production. Presses like ours should have three times the output we do. Everything is the fault of the press, or the ink, or the paper, or the humidity, or the guy on the last shift who isn't around to defend himself. Do they know how to do their jobs, or not?"

"What we really need is someone who can sort out all of this frustration and confusion and just tell us what to do, clearly and simply."

This last suggestion caught the attention of the new manager. It appealed to the part of his personality that wanted to save someone, and it gave him permission to indulge in a good old fashioned power binge.

The new manager decided the only way to stop the financial hemorrhaging was to get the order-in, order-out schedules under control—fast. He presented his Grand Solution one morning before the shift started, complete with charts on the wall, timers at workstations, and new forms. Oh, those forms—they were jewels of intricate checks and cross-checks!

All that was required to make the new system work was to change everyone's way of doing things, all at once.

You can guess what happened. The order takers made a valiant, but futile, effort to comply, proving to themselves along the way that the new forms made a bad system worse. The production workers were confused, so they broke their timers, spilled ink on, lost, accidentally threw away, or otherwise sabotaged the forms that did make it to their work stations, or "got stupid" about the forms so they were never completed the same way twice. The folks at the end of the process—the cutters and bindery people—never had a chance to try to work the new system at all; they were the angry recipients of everyone else's problems.

Is this the way to make changes to reconcile performance gaps? Did the new manager just push the process of change too fast, fewer than the workers could adapt?

No, speed was not the problem. Other companies have made wholesale changes in their systems over a weekend— but, of course, they could only do this if they were properly prepared. This new manager's problem was that he chose to act alone, without the support of his workers. His solution was a poor solution because it failed to incorporate the suggestions of the workers who knew better.

Imagine that the new manager had listened carefully to all the workers' ideas, included these ideas in his solution, but presented the plan in the same way. Would the outcomes have been any different? In the end, probably not. He still would be fixing "their" problem with "his" solution, instead of fixing "our" problem with "our" solution. By failing to include the workers in the decision-making process, the new manager denied himself smooth, rapid, and successful implementation of any plan. Even if it had been technically superior to anything else the workers had suggested, the new manager's solution was doomed because it was being forcefed to the workers.

How different would the results have been if he had said something like this?

"Thank you for all of your ideas. I've carefully thought about all of them. Now let me tell you what my ideas are and explain what I propose to do to solve our problem. You'll see that I've tried to use the best ideas, no matter who came up with them. You may not agree with my decisions initially, but

I want to explain how I arrived at them. If I've missed something, or if you foresee new problems, this is your opportunity to put your thoughts on the table so we can discuss them.

"Please give me your feedback on this plan. Our future performance depends on all of us understanding and believing in this solution. I need your help to think it through, make it the best we can do, and then implement it."

This approach empowers the workers. It demonstrates respect for the workers' abilities and knowledge, and demonstrates that the manager values their contributions to the group's performance goals.

With this approach, the workers have a much better appreciation for why the plan is the way it is. They understand the substance of it better, and they understand the thinking behind it that links it to other aspects of the company about which they may not have first-hand knowledge. They are more likely to believe in it, and adopt it as their own. Most importantly, they are likely to take the initiative and make the right decision when they encounter a problem. In this scenario, there are no bad guys—everyone is on the side of better performance.

Note that the manager in this example would not have to give up any decision-making power in order to successfully make changes. Sharing power is not a "net zero" equation that requires someone to give some up in order for someone else to get some.

Note also that extra damage the manager probably did to his Grand Solution by first presenting his approach as one of facilitation-through-empowerment, then reverting to the old-style controlling approach. His initial discussions created an expectation that he would listen and consider the workers' input; he made matters worse by talking the empowerment talk, but not walking the walk.

Empowerment Is Unique in Every Workplace

How empowerment looks and sounds in your workplace depends on your workers' willingness to get involved in the process, your level of confidence in their abilities, and the general level of trust between you and your workers.

For example, your workers may be used to having a wide latitude to select solutions and spend money to get them implemented, or they may need continual and close supervision. You may include your workers in all decisions or just some of them. In some companies, the workers are sophisticated enough to direct their own work teams, including making the hiring, firing, and compensation decisions. In other companies, the manager still makes all the final decisions.

Think about your experience with this, before you became a manger. When your boss compared your actual performance with your expected performance, how did you react? Defensive? Of course. Angry? Embarrassed? Sure. When it came time to decide how to get your performance level up to where it should be, did your boss tell you what to do, or did he or she listen to your ideas about how to do it? What approach worked best with you?

Intuitively, you know that a manager has only a narrow and limited capability to make a worker improve performance against his or her will, even when the manager has the power to punish ("Do it right the next time or I'll fire you!") and to reward ("Your work is so good, I'm giving you a raise!"). When a reluctant worker does not want performance to improve, it won't, period.

Empowered workers, on the other hand, are ready and willing to continuously seek more efficient and more effective ways to do their work. They feel some measure of control over their work, so they act on their natural desires to do the right thing and to do the best they can.

Facilitators Foster Empowerment

The manager-as-facilitator empowers workers to gain their commitment to superior performance. What does this generally look like and sound like out on the shop floor? It could be described as powersharing; or to put it another way, sharing the power to make decisions.

But empowerment is not as simple as sitting down at the weekly staff meeting and saying, "Gee, this low performance problem has really got me stumped. Poof! All of you are hereby empowered. Now the problem is yours; let me know when you've solved it."

You can't just talk your employees into behaving in an empowered way. You can't cajole them into it, or pay them more money to do it, or even train them to do it. What if they don't trust you or the company to support their decisions? What if they suspect that you will be second-guessing them, or withholding crucial information, or stepping in at the last minute to grandstand for the benefit of your ego? What if they don't trust themselves to make the right decisions?

Decision-making power is not simply given to or forced upon a person; it must be offered and accepted. Power is shared within the interpersonal relationship that is built over time between manager and worker.

The following characteristics are found in manager-worker relationships that support empowerment. These are the building blocks of empowerment:

Agreement. Agreement is the degree of similarity between a manager's and a worker's expectations, perceptions, and meanings. Since each comes to the relationship with different needs, values, and experiences, it is not surprising that precise agreement is rare. Try this eye-opening exercise: Survey each of your workers with a half-dozen questions about who in your department has the authority to do such-and-such, who are the best qualified workers for particular tasks, how they would describe the duties of five jobs they are familiar with, and how they would describe five employees within the company (e.g., "open and accessible," "level-headed," etc.). Then, before you look at the answers of your employees, answer the questions yourself. You will almost certainly be surprised with the lack of similarity in your answers—it typically ranges about 50 percent agreement.

Because each person has a different background, dissimilar views and interpretations of the same situation occur. For instance, one worker may view a shutdown of a piece of equipment as a good example of preventative maintenance; a co-worker may see the same shutdown as an overly cautious, unnecessary delay that will cause costly bottlenecks and interruptions throughout the plant.

The higher the perception of agreement between worker and manager, the higher the sense of security and satisfaction, and, ultimately, the more likely it is that a worker will take the risks associated with empowerment. She doesn't mind taking a risk if she perceives a high level of agreement between herself and her manager.

Accuracy. How accurately do you understand the differences between your viewpoint and those viewpoints of your workers? The more accurately you can describe the differences between you, the closer you are to fostering empowerment. You should be at least able to predict the others' attitudes or opinions on a subject. You should also realize that the others correctly perceive your position, even if they don't agree with you. This enables you and your workers to "agree to disagree" and thereby avoid serious conflict based on erroneous assumptions.

Serious conflicts occur when you and a worker assume you agree when you do not, or when you assume you disagree and you do not. If you disagree with each other and you both understand it, you can each make allowances for the other's point of view. But if one of you is inaccurate about the other person's viewpoint, and expects it to be the same as your own, the stage is set for conflict.

Disagreements are not necessarily bad. If you and a worker disagree, and you are both accurate about why you disagree, you each have the benefit of another perspective on the same situation. This may be very desirable when it comes to brainstorming about new initiatives, problem solving, and making decisions.

Respect. Respect is a byproduct of agreement, accuracy, and sufficient time to interact. The more you understand about the person you disagree with, the more you can respect his or her viewpoint. Hopefully, respect is a bonus of long discussions about disagreements; you may never agree, but you will at least come to respect the ideas and thought process of each other.

Trust. Trust is the result of experience working with another person. It is earned over time. It is the confidence that a worker will speak, act, and behave in a manner that is consistently honest and predictable, based on your prior experience with him. This is why day-to-day interactions are so important—they are the "little things" which are actually opportunities to practice trusting each other.

Inclusion. A sense of belonging, of being part of the group, is critical to empowerment. If a worker is shunned at break time, if he is excluded from jokes (or, worse yet, is made to feel victimized by jokes), if he is not invited to participate in formal or informal group activities (staff meetings, softball teams), he will correctly conclude that he is outside the group.

Minimally, you can expect communication between those who are "in" and those who are "out" of the group to become strained and contrived, severely limiting agreement, accuracy, respect, and trust. In addition, it is natural for those who are excluded to feel anger, shame, alienation, distrust, confusion, and lack of confidence, all of which leads to attitudes of low participation and low risk (e.g., "Why should I do anything to help them?"). As the manager, it is up to you to make sure everyone is getting an equal opportunity to contribute, even though you cannot mandate how workers treat each other. You cannot control relations between peers, but you can do much to create a work environment that at least includes everyone fairly in your meetings.

Information sharing. Information is power, no matter where you sit in the corporate hierarchy. By sharing lots of relevant information with your workers, you prepare them to participate in the decision-making process. You also demonstrate your trust in their decision-making ability and respect for their judgment. Simply knowing some of the details that cross your desk, such as monthly sales figures, year-to-date profitability, and so on, also go a long way to reducing uncertainty and boosting morale.

By adopting communication strategies that are open and honest, you foster attitudes of cooperation and collaboration. You can do this by deciding early what types of information you are prepared to share regularly with your workers, and then do it. Consistency is usually more important than completeness. Devise a memo, meeting, letter, or other format that is easy to maintain and allows for questions and feedback. Initially, your workers may not know what to do with the information you provide them, but after they see that you are consistently providing it and soliciting their input, they will begin investing time to study it, think about it, and give you their input.

Empowerment Does Not Come Easily

By now, you may believe that everyone sees the advantages of empowering workers so they can help facilitate performance improvement. Not true. If you are an autocratic leader, you may even worry that once you let the genie of empowerment out of the bottle, you may never be able to control the process again. Give them a little opportunity for input, you think, and before you can say, "Wait, that's not what I meant!", they want to run the company.

Perhaps surprisingly, empowerment does not come that easily for most people. Not everyone welcomes the added responsibility and complexity to their jobs, even if the job becomes more fulfilling in the process. You have to promote it, and make a bone-deep commitment to making it a part of your culture, even if it takes years to develop.

Some employees will continue to view empowerment as too risky, no matter what you say or do, and no matter how long they see others participate, They are satisfied to take direction, confident that if they keep you satisfied, they will get to keep their job.

Some employees will be cynical and suspicious. It's fine if your department is allowing empowered workers to participate in the decision-making process, but what about the rest of the company? What are the chances that two distinct cultures—one facilitating, one controlling—can coexist? And how do they sort out the mixed messages they receive—some supportive, some not—about their involvement?

Some workers will resist change just because it is change. Resistance to change is a daunting, stubborn obstacle to performance improvement. It is natural and pervasive. It may be active resistance from individual workers who cannot or will not develop new work habits, and it may be general, passive resistance throughout an organization bound by tradition and well-practiced procedures. Resistance can come in the form of a single order clerk who cannot (or will not) adopt the new and improved order-picking procedure. It can also come in the form of wholesale mutiny when you try doing something in a way that does not fit the corporate culture.

For some, it's easier to be cynical and skeptical than to accept the challenges of being empowered. All the excuses, all the finger pointing, all the winks and eye-rolling are simply self-defense measures from workers who believe they cannot really affect the performance improvement process.

Ask a worker why he hasn't been able to meet the expected performance standards, and you might hear some of the following:

He may say something like this:	*Because he's afraid to say this:*
"The new way of doing it is ridiculous."	"I don't understand it," or "I am not convinced this is the right way to do it."
"I didn't have enough time (or help or the right equipment)."	"I am confused and uncertain about exactly what is expected of me, so I am avoiding the goal while I try to figure it out," or "I have not accepted the need to change yet, so I am not initiating anything."

He may say something like this:	*Because he's afraid to say this:*
"You can't expect changes like these to happen overnight."	"I do not believe that you, my manager, are really going to support me in my efforts to improve my performance. The first time I make a mistake, wham—I'll be penalized and humiliated just like before," or "This new program is just another management fad. It's this month's way of getting us to worker harder," or "I am afraid of changing because I'm afraid of failing."
"It's not my fault, it's theirs."	"I feel left out of the group. I'm a loner, and I have to look out for myself."
"Who really cares, anyway?"	"I've lost my pride in my work," or "I don't know how well or poorly I'm doing now, so why take a risk and change something? It will just make me feel more uncomfortable," or "I feel unappreciated, so I've stopped trying."

Managers have a difficult time admitting they are part of the problem, too, so they tend to get defensive and blame someone else.

Empowerment does not come easily. Your employees may not be willing or able to accept expanded responsibilities; likewise, your organization may not fully support empowered workers. Nevertheless, the old rules, the rules used by the manager-as-controller, have to be updated.

Empowerment is a new rule that essentially says, "The best ideas win." To build this into your relationships with your workers, you give them plenty of opportunities and encouragement to participate and contribute. Ask them what they think, then really listen. Give them permission to throw out a half-baked idea without the fear of ridicule. Do a little cheerleading when they take the initiative and make a decision on their own. Back them up when they make a decision, even if they are wrong, provided they made the best decision they could and learned something from the experience.

THE MANAGER AS A COACH

Managing in the workplace is not unlike managing on the playing field. Your workers expect you to tell them what you expect them to do. They expect you to train them and prepare them to be successful in their attempt to meet your expectations. Finally, they expect ongoing feedback as they develop so that they can continually improve their performance.

Of course, the workers still do the work, just like the players play the game. Good managers and coaches prepare and develop their workers and players in ways that enable and empower them to achieve the preset performance standards—in other words, to win.

Imagine your favorite team, and then think about how the coach makes the team successful. The coach trains, develops, and reinforces the behavior of the players on the team. He or she teaches the skills and drills, then provides the direction and encouragement that will hopefully win the game. The coach also clearly communicates his or her expectations for the players' performance. The more specifically he or she communicates those expectations, the more likely the players will meet or exceed the coach's performance standards.

After performance expectations have been set and communicated, the worker (or player) goes to work and does his or her job. On the shop floor (or playing field), the worker (or player) is trusted to think, decide, and act largely independently, based on the manager's (or coach's) help beforehand. Later, the manager (like a coach) evaluates the worker's performance and provides feedback about it. This requires more clear communication about performance.

If performance is acceptable, there is no need to change the work (or game) plan. But if actual performance is significantly higher or lower than the established performance standard, the manager (or coach) must take action by either improving performance or revising his or her performance expectations. Improved performance may be achieved by reassigning personnel to new tasks, providing new training, or taking similar measures. Doesn't this description of the facilitation process look familiar?

APPLYING FACILITATION

If the manager of a customer service department observed a lower-than-expected rate of calls handled per day, how might he respond? He could give his workers more training, or give them incentives to work faster, or provide them with faster or better equipment, or change the makeup of the customer service teams. Or, he could lower his expectations and revise the performance standards (and his plans) to reflect the actual performance the customer service representatives were able to muster.

The important point to remember is that he must do something to make the actual performance match the expected performance specified by the objectives in the work plan. Somehow, he must facilitate a change in either the performance or the plan. If he doesn't, the work plan ceases to be a reliable planning tool. How can he plan his budget or staffing requirements if he is using performance standards that he knows his people cannot meet? The plan must be kept updated as the management cycle repeats itself so the planning function remains credible and useful.

The facilitating function is an excellent feedback and forecasting tool. Effective performance standards, coupled with monitoring and measuring mechanisms in the plan, alert the manager of problems before they occur or before they become too serious to correct. By comparing actual performance to planned performance, problems with scheduling, delivery of raw materials, quality, budgeting, production volumes, and the like are readily apparent. If the manager can see a problem developing 30 or 60 days longer in the future, he or she may still have enough time to take correct action. Likewise, if a new idea or star employee is performing better than expected, the appropriate reinforcement can be provided while there is still enough time to maximize this type of opportunity. In short, controls help managers avoid expensive surprises.

Let's take a close look at three steps of facilitating and see their effects.

Step One: Review the Planned Performance

In order to know whether a performance gap exists, you have to start with performance expectations, or standards, decided on during the planning function. Standards provide a reference point against which performance can be measured. Without clearly understanding what is expected before the work is started, neither the manager nor the subordinate will know what is acceptable performance. In other words, without standards, how can an employee's performance be evaluated? To what would it be compared? The setting of meaningful standards is an important link between the facilitating and planning functions.

Quantifiable standards are the most useful. Standards expressed in terms of costs, revenues, products produced, time to compete, net profit, unit sales, dividends, and the like are easily monitored by the manager and the worker. Target numbers and time frames can be attached to standards. Interim standards can usually be devised, too, such as "Finish the initial design phase of the new building by the first of next month," or, "Complete the inventory and restocking phase by Friday."

Performance standards may be written into work objectives in any meaningful way that is specific and measurable, such as the following: "assemble an average of 17 units per hour"; "bring the finished report to the Wednesday morning staff meeting;"; "survey 10 miles per day"; "reduce spoilage by 5 percent."

Another example: If you managed a customer service department, you may set an objective like this: "To service 50 customer inquiries per customer service representative per day"; or, an equally useful objective would be: "To meet and greet every customer entering the customer service department within 15 seconds, and to begin filling out their Request for Satisfaction form within five minutes." This is the standard of performance you expect; it is a specific, measurable outcome.

The worker should be able to track his or her own progress relative to the performance standards; there should be no doubts about "how am I doing?" In this way, the worker can direct his or her own efforts, and performance problems become self-correcting. When the standards highlight key control points in the work flow, both the manager and the worker can identify major deviations in performance before they become expensive mistakes.

Some situations defy quantifiable standards, however. As work becomes less technical and more dependent upon the employee's judgment (e.g., customer service work), it becomes increasingly difficult to find objective criteria to represent the work in a meaningful way. What standard do you use when there is literally more than one right answer? How can a service technician's or office worker's performance be evaluated if they do countless one-of-a-kind tasks throughout the day without minute-to-minute supervision? You may have to settle for imprecise measurements that relate indirectly to the performance standard, such as a survey of internal or external customers served by the technician or office worker.

Standards are most meaningful when they are set with input from those whose performance is being measured. This is especially true when you are trying to measure the unmeasurable. The employees doing the work are likely to have sound suggestions for the best control points. They also will be more confident that the evaluation process is fair if they take part in its construction.

Step Two: Evaluate the Actual Performance and Ask, Is There a Performance Gap?

You evaluate the performance of your workers by comparing their actual performance to the standards established during the planning stage. Is there a performance gap? Is the deviation from the plan large enough to merit corrective or reinforcing action? Fair evaluation depends on the accurate measurement of actual performance in the same manner specified by the standards. In other words, actual performance should be expressed in the same terms and units as the standards.

People do not perform their jobs with machine-like consistency, so the measurements and comparisons will frequently vary from the standard by a slight amount. Most of the time, this small variance will not have any effect on the end result and should be overlooked. The amount of the acceptable variation is called the *tolerance*.

For example, the manager of an overnight photo processing service may expect 100 percent of all orders in by 5:00 P.M. to be ready for customer pickup by 10:00 the following morning; if he is satisfied when 95 percent of the orders are ready, he allows a five percent tolerance. The supervisor on a packaging line may set 50 units per minute as the standard, but will allow a variance or tolerance between 47 and 53 units.

By accepting work within predetermined tolerances, the manager acknowledges that circumstances beyond the employees' control can skew short-term performance. Experienced managers know that no one can be uniformly consistent all the time. Instead of wasting time analyzing minor deviations of no consequence, they apply the exception principle, which focuses their attention on those situations with particularly good or particularly bad performance.

When performance is less mechanical and less specific, it is more difficult to measure. This is particularly true with milestones or benchmarks for work in progress, which can be subjective and indistinct. A research technician or advertising designer, for example, may find it impossible to judge how far from the correct answer or correct design he is. He may know how many experiments he's tried and how many hours he has put into the project, but he cannot say whether he is one-third or three-quarters of the way toward the solution. This difficulty occurs often enough in most organizations to be a problem, thus reinforcing the trend toward selecting more quantitative standards in the planning stage whenever possible.

Step Three: Close Any Performance Gaps by Reconciling the Difference Between Actual and Expected Performance

After actual performance is compared to the standards set up in the original plan, the manager decides if there is a performance gap worth discussing. If the actual results meet or exceed the planned results, the decision is easy: compliment the employee on a job well done and give him or her some well-deserved recognition.

If the superlative performance continues, as it might with the proper reinforcement, the manager should analyze the reasons behind the success. Perhaps the employee has developed a new technique that can be taught to others doing the same job; or, perhaps the difference is because of improved tools or new component parts or simply a better attitude toward the work. The only risk in this situation is spoiling the good performance with indifference or unwarranted meddling. By not acknowledging the good performance or by "fixing something that isn't broken," the employee may believe that extra effort doesn't matter and return to mediocre performance.

On the other hand, if performance is below expectation, the manager is obliged to do some information gathering. The beginning of the information-gathering process is the best time to involve the empowered worker.

Failure to achieve desired results cannot be automatically presumed to be the fault of the employee. Was the plan sound, or was it asking for too much in too short a time? Were the standards realistic, or were they "best guesses" based on unrelated experiences or insufficient information? Did the person assigned to this task have all the time and resources originally allocated to him or her or did someone else's assignment conflict and cause a scheduling problem? Was he or she given the leadership and motivation needed? Did he or she understand the importance of the project and have an opportunity to communicate with the rest of the team assigned to this project? What decisions did he or she make, and what was the reasoning behind them?

Obviously, the manager's information-gathering efforts are going to be more successful if the worker is involved. The experienced manager will be positive and constructive in this discussion. It is possible that something happened that made meeting the performance expectations more difficult than originally planned. A worker's failure to communicate problems that made the plan unworkable is a very different problem than failure to perform.

The prudent manager will keep in mind that the long-term objective is not to assign blame, but to accomplish the original objectives. This employee is probably going to be the one finishing the assignment after the plan is modified. If he is treated fairly by the manager, his attitude and performance will be much better.

Once the cause of the performance gap is identified, corrective actions can be taken. Ideally, the manager can control the cause of the problem and bring the performance back into line to match the original plan. One corrective technique to start with is simple feedback to the employee. Describing, but not evaluating, the performance gap to the employee responsible often makes enough of an impression to correct the problem. This nonjudgmental feedback is one form of performance counseling.

Other corrective actions may work, too. Additional or remedial training can correct skill deficiencies; tools and equipment can be repaired or upgraded; motivational techniques can be tried; or new people with more experience can be assigned to do the work.

Remedies like this will not always work, however, because many circumstances are beyond the manager's control. Late deliveries of materials by outside vendors, strikes, poor marketing results, a downturn in the economy, or pressure from a new competitor are examples of circumstances beyond the control of the manager that can have a negative affect on employee performance. In these situations, the manager must change the plan to reflect new performance expectations.

Other Characteristics of Meaningful Performance Standards

Performance standards are not developed without thoughtful consideration, tests, and lots of input from the workers affected. They are unique in every organization, and they only become meaningful when they are applied in ongoing discussions about performance.

The two most important characteristics, quantifiability and tolerances, were discussed above. Other important characteristics that make performance standards meaningful will now be listed.

Information availability and pertinence. The only information collected about performance should be the information necessary to make performance improvement decisions. The information collected should be readily available to the workers who need it to make decisions and correct their performance. Too much information or the wrong type of information is paralyzing. The manager and workers must decide early in the planning process what information should be collected. Collecting information that will not be used in any meaningful way is wasted effort and an administrative nightmare.

Timely feedback. Prompt reporting of performance data gives you and your workers the best opportunities to respond and update the planning process. In addition, all the participants will feel more confident and involved in the process if they receive timely feedback.

Flexibility. As performance gaps are identified and discussed, the plan is updated. Likewise, the performance expectations must also be updated. In the first plan, for example, performance expectations, may be tied to a budget. This would provide a valuable link to the financial plan, and it would be easy for a worker to monitor.

Upon review of the actual performance, however, it may be learned that an additional reporting tool, like an expense record, is needed. Ultimately, upon subsequent reviews of performance, a worker and manager may decide that other ways of describing performance expectations are more meaningful, such as financial ratios, quality control reports, behavior analyses, break-even point analyses, what-if financial projections, milestone schedules, critical path charts, program evaluation and review technique (PERT) charts, strategic control points, or others. Complete explanations of these tools and techniques can be found in management textbooks.

What is important to remember is that it is the manager's responsibility to have performance standards in place at the time the plan is agreed upon, then hold the worker accountable for meeting the performance expectations and finally, to reconcile the two when a significant performance gap is identified.

Chapter Eight

Communicating About Performance

The managerial skills we've discussed so far—planning, organizing, influencing, and facilitating—improve the organization's productivity and profitability. These four managerial skills can get most people doing mostly acceptable work. But by themselves, they are not enough. These skills will only yield modest success until you use your one-to-one interpersonal communication skills to talk with your people about their performance. Look at the Performance Improvement Model again in Figure 2–1. (See page 30.) Do you see how the communication skills support and link the other skills?

You communicate about performance throughout the processes of planning, organizing, influencing, and facilitating. Your communication skills lubricate and link together all of these processes, making your push towards improved performance more or less effective.

In your position, you hold a lot of power to affect the performance of your people. What you say and don't say about their current performance, both good and bad, will determine their future performance. You should regard every discussion you have about performance as an opportunity to develop your people.

Communicating about good performance is surprisingly difficult, perhaps because we believe that we should only speak up when someone does something wrong, fearful that anything we say will jeopardize the status quo. We are much more used to catching someone doing something bad than catching them doing something good.

Communicating about poor performance is also difficult. It means giving someone bad news ("I'm sorry, this is not working out"), making the person feel uncomfortable ("You lied to me, and I want an explanation"), or even telling him or her to grow up ("Your irresponsible behavior is causing a problem. This has to stop now.")

No matter how difficult it is, communicating about performance is one of your most important jobs because people want and need to know how they are doing, clearly and fairly, so they can continue to learn and grow.

YOUR RESPONSIBILITIES

As the leader of your work group, it is your responsibility to direct your employees and maximize their work efforts. Your opinion means a lot to them; make the most of the opportunities you have to guide them. The managers rated highest by employees are those who help them become the best they can be.

You now have a large responsibility for the success of your employees. Their jobs and careers depend on how well you rate their performance. How much they develop, and whether they develop at all, depends on the quality, honesty, and frequency of your feedback. This is a wonderful opportunity for you to help them develop.

You have three chief formats or platforms from which you can provide feedback:

- Informal feedback about performance (often called coaching or counseling conversations).
- Formal feedback about performance (often called performance reviews).
- Evaluations and recommendations about the readiness of an employee for advancement, a raise, a transfer, new assignments, etc., that help the company best use the skills and abilities of this person.

The bottom line, then, is that you are in the best position to evaluate, and therefore improve, your employees' performance because you can provide lots of informal and formal feedback. The best way to do this is within the context of a performance management system, either the company's or one of your own design.

You will know your performance management system is effective if it enables you to do the following.

Stay in touch. Much of your feedback about performance will be informal communication, both verbal and written. A performance management system provides you with some of the language and tools that will make this communication easier and more clear. For example, you can request an employee to join you for "an informal performance discussion about the Allied project" without sending confusing signals. An informal discussion is usually an off-the-record update of work in progress, but it is more serious than a casual conversation at the water cooler.

Stay organized. Are you meeting with your people frequently enough? You should have at least one formal performance review every year, preferably two. If you are supervising six to eight people, you may be conducting a formal review with someone every three or four weeks.

Document progress. It's difficult to track improvement and development if you don't write it down. Select or devise an evaluation form that meets your need to document performance objectives and progress toward these objectives. Then, when you meet with an employee, you will be able to discuss specific performance problems or improvements. It is likely that you will use these records to make your case for giving this person a raise, an award, or a promotion. Pay particular attention to what you are measuring. Remember, "That which gets measured gets improved." (Rule 18 of the Management Game, Chapter 14.)

Document problems. If performance improvement is not forthcoming, you will need a paper trail that documents your efforts to give the employee ample opportunity to correct the problem. Disciplinary actions, termination, not giving a raise, not promoting—you will have to defend all of these decisions, and it will be much easier to explain your reasoning if you are well-documented.

Develop the employee. This is the greatest benefit of a performance management system because it helps you and your employee plan his or her development. Right there, in black and white, is the plan that both of you understand and believe in. It highlights strengths and weaknesses, priorities for performance improvement, career objectives, whatever will be meaningful to both of you. It will serve as a trusty compass when either of you are tempted to become distracted or pursue a conflicting objective.

SUGGESTIONS FOR GIVING FEEDBACK

Because it is unreasonable to expect an employee to improve his performance when he thinks his performance is acceptable, you have to let him know otherwise. Providing feedback about performance lets a person know how well he or she is doing his or her job.

To provide feedback is to let a person know the results of his or her behavior. Feedback is a fair and clear discussion, and it is used to correct negative behavior and reinforce or support positive behavior. Giving feedback helps your employee develop the more objective self-understanding necessary for positive action and personal growth.

You have to do some preparation to give feedback. You must be ready to describe the problem and talk about its importance. You want to have some ideas about how to actively involve the employee in the solution to this problem. Your tone must be supportive and collaborative.

You have several objectives when you give feedback:

- You want to bring about behavior change.
- You want to impress upon the employee the seriousness of the situation.

- You want to elicit from the employee whatever information he/she might have.
- You want the employee to understand clearly the nature of your concerns and your commitment to resolving those concerns.
- You want to arrive at solutions to the problem.

To achieve these objectives, you will need to both give and receive feedback to achieve the greatest possible exchange of information and views.

For feedback to be effective, this one-to-one performance discussion must have the following characteristics:

- Mutual trust (confidentiality, fairness, objectivity).
- Recognition that the performance discussion is a mutual exploration to arrive at a solution.
- Two-way listening.
- Supportive behavior on your part to make it easier for the employee to talk.

In this type of an environment, feedback on any of the following behaviors can lead to remedies for performance problems:

- Discrepancies between statements and actions, verbal and nonverbal expressions.
- Distortions of self, job responsibilities, relationships.
- Evasion or avoidance of issues.
- Impact on others.
- Perceptions of strengths, weaknesses, and resources.
- Adequacy of functionality of coping behaviors.
- Defensive or manipulative behaviors.
- Appropriateness of responses to stress or conflict.

The following guidelines will help you keep your feedback constructive. Remember, this is an opportunity for development.

Limit your emotional response. In his book, *The One Minute Manager,* management consultant Ken Blanchard cautions against dwelling on your disappointment over someone's less-than-satisfactory performance. He recommends that you state your feelings clearly, just once and without discussion, and then focus on solutions. It is important to convey how you feel about what happened, but after you have made your point, move on. There is nothing to be gained by beating the employee over the head again and again with your disappointment.

Focus on a person's behavior, not his or her self-esteem. For example, say "You've been late getting back from lunch three times this week," rather than, "You like to socialize too much."

Be descriptive, not judgmental. Report your observations of what has occurred and let the employee use the feedback as he or she sees fit. When you use judgmental language, you label someone as good or bad, right or wrong. This will make any of us defensive and block communication. For example: "I have noticed . . ." or "I am concerned about . . ." or "You didn't finish the report . . ." is descriptive, but, "Your trouble is . . ." is judgmental.

Be specific, particularly about time and events. "Last week's report contains two errors" is a fact that can be dealt with; "You didn't seem to care about the work" is too vague to be useful.

Deal with the effect and do not try to imply what caused it. Talk about what you know, not what you suspect. For example: "Several letters had to be retyped" is more helpful than "You must have been too upset by something to concentrate."

Use qualifiers and avoid all-or-nothing language. "Sometimes you rush through your work and quality suffers" is going to move the discussion forward; "You never take the time . . ." or "You always rush . . ." will set up barriers between you.

Give feedback as soon as it is appropriate. Bringing up something that happened three months ago is probably too late; starting a discussion on the warehouse floor while the rest of the work group is listening is too soon.

Focus on the controllable and the changeable. Wish lists like this do not help: "If you just had not done that . . ." and "With fewer health problems. . . ." Find the workable options and don't dwell on the factors that are beyond control.

Do not demand change. You can't force someone to do something he or she doesn't want to do, so don't try. "I've told you what is wrong, so change," will only yield temporary results at best. People don't change for you, they change for themselves. "This is what will happen if this disruptive behavior continues . . ." places the responsibility for deciding to change where it needs to be.

Share ideas and information, rather than advice. Help your employees make the right decisions by providing information and sparking new ideas. You will cause more permanent change by saying something like, "It may be helpful to try . . ." or "Have you thought about . . ." than if you say, "What you ought to do is. . . ."

Share something of yourself. No one likes to talk to someone who has all the answers, has never been confused, or has never struggled with similar problems. Your relationships with your employees will be richer and more productive, meaning that you will really listen to each other more, if you let others know that you have feelings, concerns, and vulnerabilities. Don't overdo it, though; save your lectures and war stories for another audience.

Check for understanding. Even well-intentioned feedback can be misinterpreted. Summarize frequently, bring each point to a conclusion as it comes up, stay on a subject until you've both spoken your mind, and rephrase what the other says just to be sure the meaning is clear. For example: "It sounds like you want me to think of new ways to report our quality checks," and "Are we both singing out of the same songbook? As I understand it, we agree that. . . ."

SUGGESTIONS FOR ASKING FOR FEEDBACK

Performance discussions are not only a fair and efficient means to deal with many of the issues that block improved productivity, but they are also an excellent opportunity to uncover new ideas, potential problems, and valuable reactions to the plans and programs you have under way.

Asking for feedback balances the tone of the discussion with your employee, too. Rather than just "getting talked at," you can make an explicit request of him or her to help you think through some aspects of working together. This adds substance to your commitment to be collaborative.

Keep in mind that giving feedback to you, the boss, will not come easy to every one of your employees. Some will be intimidated ("Gee, he/she's the boss—what can I say that will help? I don't want to sound like an idiot."); some will be confused ("What does she want from me?" or "He's the boss—why is he asking me?"); and some will not know what to do with the opportunity ("Oh, boy, this is my opportunity to blow off steam and tell him everything that I think ought to be changed in the data processing department.").

Following are some techniques that will increase both the quantity and quality of the feedback you receive.

Ask more open-ended questions and fewer closed-ended questions. Questions beginning with words like do, will, would, is, and are tend to invite yes or no responses. "Is that clear?" and "You know whom to call, don't you?" will most likely generate one-word responses.

Open-ended questions begin with the words who, what, where, why, and how. Questions beginning with these five words tend to bring out more information because they are difficult to answer with a simple yes or no. Compare the following examples with the closed-ended questions above: "What questions do you have?", "How can I clarify that?", and "Who will you call for the information?"

Ask "suppose" questions. Suppose questions require the listener to place himself in someone else's position and respond as they think that other person should. For example, "If it were your problem, how would you handle it?" is a typical "suppose" question.

Echo. Echoing is the repetition of a speaker's words. Followed by a pause, it encourages the speaker to elaborate on that point. For example: "You feel I'm not being fair?"

Reassure. Reassure the speaker that you empathize with him or her because you have been in a similar situation or had similar feelings yourself. For example, you might say, "The end of the year is rough. I remember how uptight I always felt until all audit reports were finished."

Reflect. Reflection is a neutral observation of the feelings you see in another person. "You seem very frustrated about this" is a reflective statement.

Listen. People say more, and they say it better, when they believe someone else is really listening to them.

Good listeners are called active listeners because they are actively, not passively, involved in the discussion. They are focused on the ideas the speaker is expressing and are choosing to filter out internal and external distractions.

The following suggestions will help you to become a more active listener:

- Be attentive to the other person, psychologically and physically.
- Paraphrase key ideas to clarify and confirm meaning.
- Ask questions, but don't interview.
- Keep the discussion on track, focused, and moving.
- Summarize the major points you think you hear.

COMMUNICATING ABOUT
GOOD PERFORMANCE

Telling someone they are doing a good job sounds easy. This is not true. We are not practiced at giving praise. Most of us have grown up hearing a lot about what we are doing wrong and very little about what we are doing right. Is it any wonder that "no feedback is good feedback" for most of us? The praise and recognition we do receive is often too little and too late, and it usually depends on an award or contest or other competitive event. Since there is only one winner, are all the rest of us losers? Of course not.

Actually, the fact that praise is so uncommon makes it just that more powerful when it is used to reward good performance. Imagine yourself on the receiving end of the following comments:

"You're doing a great job, and I want to let you know we appreciate your contributions to this."

"Thank you."

"Thank you for (coming up with that solution, staying late to finish, staying with the job until it was finished, even though it was something you didn't like to do, caring enough to do it right, being here on time every day)."

"What you do is very important to the next group down the line. Because you're such a stickler for quality, they have an easier time with their part and the whole operation runs more smoothly."

"Your suggestion has saved us time and money. Thank you, and here is (a bonus, a complimentary ticket, a certificate, a round of applause) to let you know that we really appreciate your help in making this a better place to work."

Get the idea? What you say is less important than how you say it. If you say it at all, and you are sincere, you will unleash the tremendous power of positive reinforcement.

Remember this: you get more of that behavior which you recognize and reward. If you want more people to come in early, start complimenting the early arrivals, keep track of arrival times, or make free donuts available. If you want to improve productivity, let everyone know how you are measuring productivity, publicize the results, and spotlight new ideas and outstanding efforts that contribute to the goal. This is basic. Your people want to do well and be recognized for their efforts because it makes them feel good about themselves. Recognize and reward good performance to get more of it.

There are many ways to acknowledge good performance. Ideally, your recognition or reward will feel right for the person and circumstance. An encouraging word is probably appropriate for work in progress, for example, while a formal public acknowledgment would be suitable for milestone results. As we discussed in Chapter 6, "Influencing Skills," different people are motivated by different rewards.

Two ways to reward a person are to give him or her a promotion and/or increased compensation. But these are obviously going to be used only infrequently. Some other ways to acknowledge good performance are:

- Awards (cash, trophy, certificate, travel, etc.).
- Recognition in the company newspaper or on the plant bulletin board.
- Increased responsibility (special projects, committee or task force leadership, United Way chairmanship, etc.).
- Special training.
- Memberships in professional or trade associations as the company representative.

Can you overpraise? Yes. This is common sense—if everything is treated as a major accomplishment, or if everything is given equal acknowledgment, people will not be motivated to push themselves to get the big results for the big recognition. Give them a taste of positive rewards at whatever level they've earned it—even if it is just for showing up for work and doing their job—and they will begin to work hard for more of it. For most people, positive feedback is its own reward because it reinforces their self-esteem.

Following are a few ways to remind ourselves to recognize and reward our employees' good performance.

1. Make a review of key productivity measurements a part of your routine. Then, generously administer compliments and other positive feedback.

2. Give your employees opportunities to talk to you casually. They will tell you what they are proud of! Purposely stand around during a break, walk around the plant, ask questions of an operator, share a story of your weekend in a relaxed manner—when you do, you signal to your employees that this is a good time to approach you.

3. Start a suggestion box. It's corny, but it's a recognized communication channel that is nonthreatening.

4. Watch for individual contributions to the corporate goals. If new account development is a priority, make a big deal out of it when your people respond with ideas and actions. Employee of the Week (or Month) programs are popular because they work.

5. Publicize progress toward the group's goals. Put your output chart up in the employee lunchroom. Help your people feel good every day about doing a good job.

Don't underestimate the power of praise. Because it encourages people to want to do well, it is more powerful than a reprimand. It is also easier to administer. As we will see in the next section, correcting behavior requires an unceasing effort to push and pull people back from that which we don't want them to do.

COMMUNICATING ABOUT POOR PERFORMANCE

It is natural to avoid conversations about poor performance because they are as uncomfortable to give as they are to receive. We don't like being judged, and we don't like feeling like we are judging someone else.

It is also natural to dislike discussions about poor performance because to do so puts us in conflict with one of our favorite myths: everything and everyone is doing well. It's human nature to give people the benefit of the doubt, excuse them, and hope the problem will take care of itself. "We've got the best people in the business," we tell ourselves. "If they can't get their work done, there must be a good reason." Realistically, you probably have your share of outstanding performers, mediocre performers, well-intentioned incompetents, and all the rest.

Communicating about poor performance is also risky for working relationships, and we don't like that, either. We are often put in situations where we must take corrective action when we are not completely prepared. Are our instincts always right, or does our unintentional bias, prejudice, lack of clear standards, lack of information about the job or the work sometimes yield an unfair evaluation of performance? If we are wrong, or handle the discussion badly, we have put a chip on the shoulder of someone we will have to work with again.

But significant performance problems inevitably creep into the work flow. The difficulty is not in identifying a performance problem, but in deciding what to do about it. Consider Doug's problem with Tricia during a recent performance discussion:

Doug

What's going on, Tricia?, I know you understand the plan for our department. You know what our objectives are, and you know we've gone to a lot of trouble to reorganize the shift schedule to accommodate everyone's needs. Up until last week, your production was good—I think you even had a shot at the Hawaii trip, didn't you?

Tricia

I suppose so. I was really excited about that.

Doug

Was? Why not now? Your production has dropped back to where it was before.

Tricia

I know. I can't really explain it, but . . .

Doug

Doggone it, Tricia, just do it. I'm going to be watching your numbers, and they better be up again by next week.

In the exchange above, Doug squandered a good opportunity to learn more about how the new process was working. He believes he has done his job, and now it's time for the employees to do theirs. But new plans, new ways of organizing, incentives, and facilitating discussions don't get the work done. That comes out of one-to-one discussions about performance. Remember that every performance discussion is an opportunity for your people to develop their skills. They learn the most on the job, and you are their best teacher.

GETTING STARTED

Let's apply some of our communication skills to approach some sample performance problems. Notice that these utilize the wide range of performance management techniques discussed earlier.

Step 1: Ask Yourself Whether There is Really a Performance Problem Here

Or, is this a communication problem? If it's a communication problem, is it possibly an issue simply because you are speaking differently (or listening differently) to a person who is different from yourself? (See Chapter 12 for a discussion about working with a diverse workforce.) Before you say anything to anyone about what you perceive is a performance problem, stop and think about what you expected to occur and what actually happened. Consider the following questions.

A. Were mutual performance expectations clearly understood?
  1. What precisely was your understanding?
  2. How, specifically, was performance to be measured? Are you still satisfied that the measurement was fair?

   3. Could this possibly be a communication problem? If it is, the problem with poor performance remains, but you will need to handle it differently.

B. What was the actual performance?

   1. Job performance that can be easily observed and measured can be described in terms of action, result, and time. Example: *Henrietta made presentations to 15 clubs and sold $100,000 worth of new orders in the past two weeks.*

   2. Job performance that is not easily observed and seldom documented is more difficult to evaluate objectively. Rather than relying on your impressions, establish specific milestones of progress within specific time frames. Example: *Warren finished the research on one-half of the cities in Michigan by the end of the week.*

   3. Job performance that is unpredictable or otherwise hard to measure must be evaluated in terms of observable behaviors, however infrequent, and their consequential results. Then, a baseline for behaviors or outcomes can be established by averaging whatever figures are meaningful over a longer time period. Example: *Thelma's public relations efforts yielded a 15 percent increased awareness of the smog problem based on the increase in the number of calls to the hot line. The increase in the number of articles longer than 250 words run in the newspapers has also been significant, although the impact is more difficult to measure.*

C. What is the difference between the actual and expected performance? Is there a performance gap?

   1. What, exactly, is the performance problem? (How long has it been a problem? When and where does it or does it not occur? How often does it occur?)

   2. Is the performance gap important? (What impact does the incorrect performance have on the quality, quantity, and cost of the product or service? What impact does the wrong performance have on the corporate image, safety, or other employees?)

3. Has this employee ever done this correctly? (If so, when? If not, has anyone ever performed this correctly? How were the circumstances similar or different?)

4. How will you know when the problem is solved? What will be different?

Step 2: Ask Yourself Whether This is a "Can't Do" or "Won't Do" Problem

Answering this question will help you understand where the difficulty originates and then select the best approach to solve the problem. Most commonly, any one or a combination of the following factors could be involved:

1. *Aptitude.* An individual with poor manual dexterity will never be able to excel at a task like typing or repairing delicate electronic equipment. Given a supportive and patient supervisor, however, he or she could possibly be brought up to an acceptable level of performance.

2. *Ability.* Some people have sufficient aptitude for a given task but their abilities have not been developed to take full advantage of their aptitude.

3. *Interest.* You have probably dealt with people who had the aptitude and ability to perform well but who, for whatever reason, simply lacked interest and performed at a level well below their capabilities.

4. *Attitude.* Doesn't a person's attitude affect his or her performance? If an individual resents authority, he or she will not respond well to directives, will probably do only what must be done and, in general, will require closer supervision than you would like.

A "can't do" performance problem exists when an employee cannot, for some reason, perform as expected. The person does not lack willingness, but does lack aptitude and/or ability.

A "won't do" performance problem exists when an employee appears to have all the resources and capabilities to perform the job or activity properly, but is not doing so. A "won't do" problem is an interest and attitude problem.

Determining whether an employee has a can't do or won't do performance problem will not make communicating about it easier, but you will at least be able to focus your discussion on potential remedies instead of excuses and defensiveness.

Step 3: Coach or Counsel Your Employee

Whether your approach is coaching or counseling, pick the right time to discuss the performance problem. You may need to address the problem immediately if there is a possibility of injury, high cost, or the creation of an even larger problem. On the other hand, you may want to wait until after emotions have cooled.

The performance discussion may be as casual as a few moments together in the hallway or at the water cooler, or it may be a closed-door conversation lasting a half-hour or longer. Pick a time and place for your discussion that will minimize distractions and anything else that could confuse the issues.

Coaching conversations are effective with "can't do" performance problems—those relating to aptitude and ability. They are generally developmental in tone and intend to train and reinforce the behavior of the employee. They are usually not held in response to a particular incident of poor performance.

The manager may initiate a coaching conversation to discuss broadening an employee's responsibilities or to address minor problems that can be resolved with instructions or new information. Coaching conversations are also used to reinforce good performance by giving the employee more frequent positive feedback about his or her behavior or results.

Coaching conversations tend to look quite far into the future: "We're going to have to get started on your development as a shift leader, Bob. You know that Frank is going to be retiring soon and we have two new drill presses on the way, so we've got to figure out a plan to get you up to speed."

The employee may initiate a coaching conversation to get additional information ("What do you think of what I did, boss?" or "How did that work?") or to give feedback to you ("Our plan didn't work quite the way we intended . . .").

Counseling conversations focus on the "won't do" problems of attitude and interest. They are usually intended to help the employee modify his or her behavior in order to achieve the results desired by the manager. They generally are intended to improve the employee's performance in a specific area. Counseling is used most often to address minor performance problems that can be resolved by communicating or clarifying consequences or incentives.

When counseling an employee, you will want to:

1. Describe the problem as neutrally and objectively as possible by using descriptive statements.

2. Indicate the impact of the problem on you, the employee's co-workers, or anyone else who is affected.

3. Probe for details from the employee's viewpoint. The employee may have information you do not have. Use open-ended questions to bring that information out and listen, listen, listen!

4. Discuss solutions to the problem. What can you and/or the employee do to correct the situation?

5. Agree on an action plan and decide when you and the employee will sit down again to review results.

Coaching and counseling conversations work because they are:

- Short—usually between 3 and 10 minutes.
- Informal—as the name suggests, they are conversational in tone.
- Typically unscheduled or arranged only shortly in advance.

Coaching and counseling conversations are private and personal. While some small group team meetings could be considered coaching conversations, most coaching and counseling conversations are held in a private, one-to-one setting.

No documentation is required, although it may be useful to jot a few notes down to use in the next formal performance review.

WHAT HAPPENS WHEN PERFORMANCE DOESN'T IMPROVE?

In spite of your best efforts, the performance of some of your employees may not improve. Eventually, you will have to decide to escalate the performance issue to resolve it, or choose to ignore it. Your options include a process of progressive disciplinary actions leading up to termination.

In the workplace, disciplinary actions mean development, not punishment. Disciplinary actions are an extension of the values we expressed earlier:

We are partners in this business enterprise.

Each of us have our jobs to do.

We are committed to each other's success.

When one of us chooses not to do his or her job, the rest of us have to choose a new partner with whom we can work.

Escalating your response to include disciplinary actions or termination is a serious decision. You and the company have an investment in the employee, and your actions from here forward put that investment at risk.

Strong disciplinary action—up to and including a discharge—on a first offense may be invoked when the employee commits a very serious violation of the company's rules. There is universal agreement that certain behaviors are totally unacceptable, such as stealing, destruction of company property, and deliberate actions that put safety at risk.

Less serious infractions, such as chronic lateness, require a progressive disciplinary response. These are problems too serious to ignore, yet are not so serious that the company has to cut its losses and terminate its investment in the employee. As manager, you must establish a specific incident or pattern of unacceptable performance before you begin a disciplinary response. Poor quality work resulting in a client complaint, for example, may happen once or many times before disciplinary action is triggered; as long as you are providing the employee with clear and consistent feedback, you can keep your options open.

IMPROVING PERFORMANCE: A PROGRESSIVE APPROACH

The most successful and fair approach to improving an employee's performance is a process of:

1. Communicating progressively more directive verbal and written messages (i.e., "You *will* finish the assignment in the warehouse by Tuesday . . .").
2. Administering progressively more negative consequences for noncompliance.

In other words, you "turn up the heat" or "raise the ante" until you get the employee's attention and cause him or her to choose to improve his or her performance. By explaining what the negative consequences of poor performance are in advance, you give the employee every reasonable opportunity to decide to do his or her job in the way that meets your expectations. When you do this, you are strongly influencing his or her development of career choices, self-control, and decision-making skills. If the employee implicitly or explicitly decides he or she does not want to work for you, his or her performance will reflect that choice.

A progressive disciplinary approach recognizes that you cannot force people to do something they don't want to do; nor can you afford to tolerate poor performance indefinitely. You may not be able to control an employee, but you can control the quantity and quality of work standards that the company finds acceptable. This approach recognizes that even though the employee may be content to drift with below-par work, you have no such luxury. You must fire such a person who has mentally quit his or her job and get someone in who can do the job right. The sooner you get a poor performer replaced, the better for everyone, including him or her.

Most of us will go to extraordinary lengths to rationalize employee behavior so we can avoid this uncomfortable and difficult process. We avoid it as long as possible because:

- We hope the problem will go away.
- We know that if we start it, we have to finish it, even when we can't "fix" the situation.
- We are afraid that the whole thing will somehow backfire.
- We just aren't sure what to do.

Except for the most serious offenses that require immediate termination, offering employees progressively more serious consequences to their actions is a preferred strategy. A progressive approach assures clear communication about the issue, ample opportunities to discuss it, and gives the employee plenty of time to change his or her behavior.

Keep in mind that you are simply providing feedback to the employee about his/her actions. You are setting the standards and communicating what is and is not acceptable performance. Based on the feedback an employee gets from you, he/she makes choices about his or her future actions. Since the process escalates only when the employee fails to change and make the necessary improvements, he/she can stop the negative consequences at any time by choosing to comply.

When you have a performance problem, your company's version of a progressive approach to discipline should include most of the following six steps:

Step 1: An informal discussion about the difference between performance expectations and actual results.

Step 2: An oral warning that performance has not improved. Documentation is placed in the personnel file for one year. It is removed if the employee's improved performance earns him/her a "clean slate."

Step 3: A written warning that becomes a part of the permanent personnel file.

Step 4: A second oral or written warning that becomes a part of the permanent personnel file.

Step 5: Suspension.

Step 6: Discharge.

Following is a description of what happens at each step.

Step 1: *The Informal Discussion*

The purpose of this step is to communicate clearly about the gap between expected and actual performance. This puts an employee on notice that there is a problem and presents the corrective action he or she must take. This is your opportunity to clear up any communication problems that may exist. Your goals are to explain the rule violated and why it exists, to uncover and resolve any problems the employee may have in meeting the rule, and to express confidence in the employee's avoiding similar situations in the future. At the conclusion of this discussion, the employee should have no doubt about what is expected of him or her.

Keep this discussion entirely off-the-record; make no notes other than those you will need to follow up on the employee's progress in a few weeks, and do not put anything into his personnel file.

Common problems that can be solved at this first step of the process are excessive lateness, absenteeism, prolonged breaks, low productivity, and inferior quality of work. Those and similar problems can frequently be resolved early. And the key to change is an effective discussion emphasizing problem solving.

Let's use Ruth and her dialogue with her supervisor as an example of how the informal discussion works. Ruth is a customer service rep who has been late three times and absent twice, including yesterday, within the past month. Ruth has been with the company for eight months and, until now, has presented no other problems, so an informal discussion seems appropriate.

The supervisor calls Ruth into her office and begins by saying:

Supervisor

Good morning, Ruth. Please sit down. I want to talk to you informally about your attendance. I'm concerned that we may have a problem, and it's beginning to affect your performance and the performance of others.

Ruth

Look, I know I've been late a couple times, but I'm not the only one . . .

Supervisor

Well, let's see. My records indicate you've been late three times and absent twice in the last month. Does that sound right?

Ruth

Yeah, I guess so. But I didn't mean to be late, and one of those absences just couldn't be helped!

Supervisor

Ruth, there's no need to get defensive. I'm just trying to solve our problem.

Ruth

Just how much trouble am I in?

Supervisor

That's going to be up to you. I want to review a couple of points with you and make our position clear, okay?

Ruth

Sure. Go ahead.

Supervisor

To start with, do you understand that to give our customers proper service, you must be available? As you know, you're always working on estimates and schedules with our customers in the eastern region. No one else can fill in for you on short notice. Maybe we should be organized differently, but we aren't right now. They start calling us at the crack of dawn, and if you aren't here to help them, they don't get the answers they need. You're an important part of our team, and you are badly missed when you aren't here.

Ruth

I understand that, of course.

Supervisor

I'm sure you do—or did. Up until a month ago, I could always rely on you to be here on time, every day. What's going on? Are you unhappy with your job?

Ruth

No, I love my job. The real problem is my husband's working hours. Until about six weeks ago, he worked the 4 P.M. to midnight shift, which means he was home during the day to look after the twins. His company changed his hours to day shift and now he has to leave at 7:00 A.M. So if the nursery school bus is late or Jimmy is sick, my husband isn't there to help.

Supervisor

This sounds like a difficult situation for you.

Ruth

It is. Even on the good days, I can just barely make it here on time. It sure makes for a hectic morning.

Supervisor

I can imagine. What do you plan to do?

At this point, Ruth became very distressed and admitted she had no solutions. It was clear to her supervisor that Ruth had unrealistic hopes that the situation would "just work itself out, somehow, someway."

Supervisor

Ruth, I can't decide for you how to solve this problem, but I want to try to help. You're a valued member of our team here, and I need you to be here on time and in the proper frame of mind to help our customers. What's keeping you from solving this problem?

Ruth

Time. I think I need to find a way to handle the twins differently in the morning, and that means talking to the day care center, other parents, maybe even my neighbors. I may have to even switch day care centers.

Supervisor

How much time do you need?

Ruth

Well, a few hours. It's impossible to do on the phone . . .

Supervisor

If I give you next Tuesday and Thursday afternoons off, would that give you enough time to find a solution?

Ruth

Gosh, I'll make it work. That would be great . . .

Ruth returned with her problem solved. Her supervisor only vaguely knows the details—Ruth now has some sort of an arrangement with a neighbor and a parents' car pool—but she doesn't even need to know that much. Ruth's supervisor is satisfied to know that this valued employee has not been late once in three weeks and has returned to her previous level of effectiveness with the customers in the eastern region.

Sound easy? Well, the supervisor applied many of the skills we've discussed. For example:

- She described the specific actions and behaviors that were becoming problems.
- She explained how Ruth's actions and behaviors were affecting performance and reviewed why it was important that Ruth meet the performance expectations.
- She encouraged Ruth to find her own solutions and supported her efforts to do so. Throughout the discussion, Ruth continued to own her problem and her responsibility, and the supervisor was careful not to get so involved with finding the solution that it would no longer belong to Ruth. (After all, she will have to make her solution work.)
- She avoided generalizations and personal attacks.
- She listened carefully, alternately echoing and leading Ruth's comments as they thought through the problem together.
- She asked open-ended questions that would elicit information.
- She reviewed and asserted her expectations for Ruth's performance.
- She expressed her understanding and sympathy of Ruth's feelings and problems.
- She was encouraging and supportive.

Sometimes the informal discussion does not bring about sufficient improvement. Or, you may need a more formal discussion sooner. In either case, use the oral warning.

Step 2: The Oral Warning

This is the first formal, documented step in a progressive disciplinary process. You will have to:

- Describe the infraction and its impact.
- Review any previous discussions you might have had, especially if they were during the past year.
- Ask the employee to explain the situation from his/her viewpoint.
- Ask how he/she will avoid recurrences.
- Agree on actions you and/or the employee will take.
- Let the employee know what disciplinary action you are now taking.
- Inform the employee that you will prepare a memo on this discussion that will be held in the files for one year.
- Advise the employee that a recurrence might result in further disciplinary action.
- Express confidence in the employee's ability to resolve the situation.
- Set a specific date for a follow-up discussion to review progress.

Following the discussion, you should prepare a file memo summarizing each of the above steps. If at the end of one year no further action has been required, the memo should be given to the employee. This helps to convince the employee that the matter is closed and that he/she now has a clean slate. It also gives you a formal opportunity to recognize the employee's successful efforts.

To illustrate, let's consider the case of John, a public utility repairmen. John's job is to respond to customer complaints about leaks, discover the source of the leak, and make necessary repairs. The department's experience has shown that about 2 percent of a repairman's calls result in call-backs—in other words, the customer calls again because the leak has not been eliminated. John seems to be having more than his share of problems.

John's manager calls him into his office to discuss the situation.

Manager

John, I want to talk to you again about the number of call-backs you've been getting. We've talked informally about this issue twice in the last three months and it's still a problem.

John

What's wrong now?

Manager

Your call-back rate is running about 4½ percent, more than twice our standard. As you know, call-backs are expensive and bad for customer relations.

John

I've just been having bad luck.

Manager

I don't think it's a matter of luck, John. The call-back reports indicate that a lack of care in doing the repairs. Last week, for example, you repaired a pinhole in a lead-in pipe by plugging the hole, but you neglected to wrap the pipe in safety tape. As a result, the plug worked loose and we got a call-back. Actions like these really count for a good part of the 4½ percent. Aside from bad luck, what other reasons do you think might account for your high call-back rate?

John

I don't know. I just think you're out to get me. You're always calling me on the carpet. The other guys make mistakes too, you know!

Manager

I realize that. I made mistakes when I was a repairman, too. John, we have to face it. You're having more problems than you should and I'd like some ideas from you on how these incidents can be avoided . . . (Pause).

John

I don't know.

Manager

Let me first suggest that you review the procedures manual. It might also help if I put you in the brush-up program.

John

Those are good ideas, but they won't help. I know the work.

Manager

Maybe it won't solve all the problems, John, but these are at least steps in the right direction. Do you have any other ideas?

John blurted out that what he really needed was a good night's sleep. "Tell me what you mean, John," said the manager. John said he had not been sleeping well because of personal problems, and this made it hard for him to concentrate day after day.

Manager

John, I don't know how to solve your problems, but this gives me an idea as to how we can solve ours. Would it help to talk to the company's employee assistance counselor?

John

The what?

Manager

The employee assistance counselor. He's trained to help you get through whatever problems you're having that keep you from doing your best work. You know—financial, emotional, drinking . . .

John

I guess I'm an old fashioned guy like my Dad. I was raised to keep my problems to myself, so I guess I just figured that I would eventually get these worked out.

Manager

You tell me. Old fashioned or not, it sounds like you could use some help. Should I set it up?

John

Geez, I don't know . . .

Manager

Let me put it this way: I think you need some help. I'm very serious about this. If your work doesn't improve, you'll leave me no choice but to take further disciplinary action. We've had informal talks in the past, but this discussion is an oral warning. I'll have to speak to the superintendent as well as write a memo documenting our discussion and place it in your personnel file. This will stay in your record for the next year. If you come up to standard and remain there, I'll be very happy to remove it from the file.

John

You're not being fair!

Manager

What's there to be fair about? You know you've been expected to change, yet you have chosen not to seek help. Now I am offering it to you again, and I'll keep getting tougher on you until you take it. Now which will it be: the EAP counselor or the retraining, or both?

John soon received the help he needed. His supervisor was satisfied that whatever was distracting him was resolved to the point where his performance returned to normal.

The oral warning differed from the informal discussion in two important ways:

1. The discussion was no longer just between the manager and the employee. The manager's superior has been notified that a problem exists.

2. The manager has, following the oral warning, placed a memo in the employee's file that summarizes the discussion.

Step 3: The Written Warning

Most disciplinary situations can be handled as informal discussions or oral warnings. The written warning, however, differs significantly in the following respects:

- The discussion may be conducted by, or in the presence of, the manager's superior to further emphasize the gravity of this step.

- Another memo will be placed in the employee's file. This time, however, it will remain there for an indefinite period of time.

- A letter of warning is also placed in the employee's file that fully describes the problem, attempts to resolve it, the employee's response, the agreed-upon plan for corrective action, the possible consequences for further poor performance, and a future date to review progress. The letter is read and given to the employee as part of the disciplinary discussion. Many organizations request the employee to sign the file copy as evidence that the employee received and understood it.

Step 4: A Second Oral or Written Warning That Becomes a Part of the Permanent Personnel File

Some organizations, particulary those that must be in strict compliance with personnel quotas to maintain their government contracts, may feel the need to take this extra step to document their efforts to be fair and reasonable with an offending employee.

Step 5: Suspension

Some organizations do not use suspension as part of their progressive discipline process. It should be considered for the following reasons:

- None of the preceding steps has imposed an economic penalty. Until that happens, some employees may not take the progressive discipline process seriously. The added pressures caused by a loss of income may finally cause a change in the employee's behavior.

- If a third party is to review an eventual discharge, the fact that no improvement took place after one or a series of suspensions will weigh heavily in the manager's favor.

Most organizations that use suspension as part of the process approach it in either of two ways: 1) a severe (three or five-day) suspension following an unsuccessful written warning, or 2) a series of suspensions, generally a one-day followed by a three-day, and finally a five-day suspension. The discussion procedures to be used at the time of suspension are the same as for the oral warning and documentation is the same as for the written warning.

Step 6: Discharge

If you have followed the preceding steps and the employee's behavior has not changed, you are left with no choice but corporate capital punishment—discharge.

By now, you have probably resigned yourself to losing this employee, but others may not be. You can avoid being reversed and having the employee reinstated by being aware of what a third party typically looks for when reviewing a discharge. When hearing a dismissal appeal, third parties basically want to be assured that you took every precaution to deal fairly with the employee. Here are some major factors they take into consideration:

- Forewarning: Can you demonstrate that the employee has been informed of your expectations, his or her performance, and any alleged performance gap? You don't have to forewarn employees that theft, willful destruction of property, drinking on the job, and other major violations of the rules are grounds for immediate dismissal. But standards regarding lateness, absences, quality of work, and similar problems do need to be communicated since expectations vary so much from one organization to another.

- Probable consequences: Employees must be informed of what may happen if their behavior continues. The choice is then theirs.
- Reasonable rules: Can you demonstrate that the rule fills a business need? And does it apply to all employees in the work unit?
- Documentation: Is it complete? Was it done at the time of your discussion?
- Penalties: Are they realistic or excessive? Were they imposed soon after the occurrence or at a later date?
- Right to appeal: Did the employee have access to higher levels of management to explain his/her views?

GUIDELINES FOR USING COMMUNICATION TO IMPROVE PERFORMANCE

Progressive disciplinary action is the approach you must use as a last resort when nothing else has been effective. Think the employee's performance problem through thoroughly. Have you done everything possible to identify and develop this employee's strengths? Have you been sincere and reasonable in finding a solution? Will your forthcoming actions be regarded as fair, or will they be a surprise and appear arbitrary? Are you prepared to lose this employee? Careful consideration of certain issues can put us in a more comfortable and confident position when we take the initial disciplinary action or when a subsequent action seems necessary. Some of the more important considerations include the following.

Timing. How much time has elapsed since the last infraction and discussion? The shorter the time span, the greater the latitude we have in moving the incident from an oral warning to a written warning. Generally, if one year has elapsed since the last infraction, you must begin the process all over again.

General performance pattern. Is this infraction part of a pattern of marginal or poor performance? Is it the first instance? If the problem is recurring and is part of a pattern, stronger disciplinary action may be appropriate. On the other hand, if this behavior is unusual for this employee, you will probably want to refrain from strong action.

Clear understanding of expectations. Are you certain that this employee is aware of the company's standards? Many supervisors, as part of their new employee orientation, make a point of sitting down with new employees and reviewing the standards and policies such as those relating to absences or breaks. This kind of discussion also offers an ideal opportunity to communicate the reasons for the expectations.

Precedent. How have similar infractions been handled in the past? Unless you can demonstrate that this situation or this employee is different, you must respond just as you would have in the past. This does not mean, however, that once a traditional response has been established it cannot be changed. To bring about change requires you to do two things: first, you should communicate the new rule to all employees; second, you should allow a reasonable time for the individuals involved to adjust their behavior. During this transition phase, you should have an informal performance discussion when an infraction occurs.

Effect on co-workers. What is the effect of this individual's behavior on other members of the work force? Your action—or inaction—almost always has an effect on other employees. Are people entitled to longer breaks, for example, when they work faster than anyone else? Are you making yourself vulnerable to possible charges of favoritism? Do your responses to problems build or tear down morale?

Special circumstances. What unique factors contributed to this situation? Personal pressures from home, changing health conditions, or a suddenly heavier workload may cause performance to slide temporarily; an employee in this position needs compassion and extra help, not more pressure.

Seniority. Seniority usually matters. The greater an employee's seniority, the more reluctant a third party will be to uphold severe disciplinary action, except in the most serious situations. It is reasonable, for example, to suspend a senior employee when a relatively new employee would be discharged for the same infraction.

Defense. If an employee appeals your action, will you be able to adequately defend yourself? Do you have evidence, witnesses, or documentation that demonstrate your action was reasonable?

How would you handle the special considerations in the following circumstances?

1. In reviewing the monthly materials waste report, you discover that Karen has waste that is almost twice the group average. She has already received an oral warning for this problem. What options do you have if the oral warning was given:
   a. 14 months ago?
   b. Last month?
   c. 11 months ago?

Your options will be customarily limited by applying the one-year rule. If at least a year has elapsed since the oral warning, it is presumed that the employee has, or had, learned her lesson and is entitled to start the disciplinary process over again with another oral warning. If the last warning was within the year, you can move to a written warning. Obviously, 11 months is borderline, and you have to consider general performance during that period and any special circumstances that might now exist in the current situation.

2. Greg and Paul were caught sleeping in a company truck by a district supervisor. Greg has been with the company 18 years and has had a very good record. Paul, however,

has been in trouble before. During his two years with the company, you have had talks with him about some of his practices, one of which led to a written warning about three months ago. Both Greg and Paul are fully aware that sleeping on duty is considered a major infraction and could result in discharge. You have decided to discharge Paul.

   a. Can you discharge Paul and not Greg?

   b. What difference does Greg's seniority make?

   c. Considering the seriousness of the infraction, what disciplinary action would seem appropriate in your dealings with Greg?

You can expect to receive some pressure to treat both men equally. But remember, your objective is to be fair, and equal treatment is not always the same as fair treatment. Whenever you decide to treat one employee differently from another, you take on the additional burden of possibly having to defend the difference in treatment. In this case, there are substantial reasons for treating Greg and Paul differently. Unlike Paul, Greg has a long history with the company and he also has a very good record. Greg's co-workers could probably see discharging him as overkill. As Greg's manager, however, you cannot avoid taking some quite severe disciplinary action with him. Suspending Greg for one or two weeks (without pay, of course) would seem to be an appropriate response.

3. For several years, it has been the practice of machine operators in your area to punch out about 10 minutes before the end of their shift. The former plant manager knew the employees who did this, but never said anything to them.

This morning, however, you received a memo from the new plant manager saying the practice had to stop, and, beginning immediately, anyone caught punching out early would be suspended for the following day. You immediately meet with the operators and read the memo to them. As a further precaution, you post the memo on the bulletin board. Ken, one of your longtime good employees, is out for the day and so does not attend the meeting.

The next day, in spite of the posted memo and your attempted intervention, Ken punches out early. You stop him as he is leaving early and tell him you have no choice but to suspend him for a day. Ken protests and says, "You know I have to leave early so I can see my wife before visiting hours at the hospital are over. Besides, everyone's been doing this for years. Give me a break. I can't afford to lose a day's pay." You point out the memo on the bulletin board and tell Ken that's the way it has to be and there can be no exceptions. Ken says he'll go to the union.

   a. What do you think the union's position will be?
   b. What considerations do you think the union will present in arguing Ken's case?
   c. How do you think the situation should have been handled?

The union will undoubtedly argue vigorously for Ken's defense, basing its case on the following points:

• Timing (Ken had not personally been told of this change and lacked forewarning.)

• Otherwise good general performance (Ken has a clear record and is considered one of the better employees.)

• Precedent (punching out early had been an acceptable practice for many years.)

• Special circumstances (Ken has a sick wife, and the visiting hour restrictions make it difficult for him to comply with the new rules.)

• Seniority (Ken has been with the company too long to be treated in this shabby and arbitrary manner.)

As Ken's supervisor, you could have handled the situation more effectively by:

• Appealing to the plant manager about the advisability of suspension beginning immediately, saying something like, "Surely this will have a negative effect on the other employees because it would be perceived as unfair; besides, how much harm has been done? What will it cost us to be lenient within the bounds of common sense?"

• Insisting that the employees be given a week or two to adjust to the new rule before formal disciplinary action be taken.

- Recommending that any infractions during the time of transition be handled by an informal discussion with the employee.

- Presenting to the plant manager Ken's situation and other cases where a person may have a legitimate reason for leaving early; then, elicit any ideas he/she has on how to handle these cases.

- Discussing the new rule with the plant manager before presenting the rule to the employees; by the time you present it, you should be able to support it, describe the reasons for it, and explain the length and purpose of the adjustment phase and what accommodations can be made for those who have special problems.

4. Annabelle has been a superior payroll clerk in most respects for eight months. Your only problem with her occurred about four months ago when she failed to complete a quarterly report before she took a few days off, making it necessary for you to call in extra help. You talked to her upon her return, but didn't want to come down too hard because she is otherwise very good at her job. In an off-handed way, you suggested she try to finish all her work before taking time off the next time. Last week, however, she mentioned on her way out the door for a three-day absence that she did not do the report again. You were upset that she left you and others to finish her work. Now that it has happened again, you are considering giving her an oral warning. During this morning's discussion, you discovered that Annabelle's interpretation of your last talk had been that you would like her to finish that report before she left if she had time, but it was not mandatory.

    a. Should you follow through on an oral warning? Why or why not?

    b. What points do you feel should be made in this discussion that were not covered in the previous talk?

Given the informality of the first talk, Annabelle obviously did not feel forewarned. She may be faulted for poor judgment, but considering that you were not specific about what you wanted done in your first discussion, her behavior was not unreasonable. Now is the time to make your expectations clear with another informal discussion. You will want to make the point that Annabelle must complete all her reports, including this one, before she takes time off. You may find it useful to point out that the reason for your insistence on this point is because of the negative consequences suffered by others when she does not complete her job.

Supervisors who follow the progressive approach—where each step becomes more serious—can feel secure about their actions. Their actions are fair and reasonable extensions of efforts to develop the employee to his or her full potential.

Disciplinary situations are never pleasant, but you can keep them in perspective if you remember that:

- Like development activities, disciplinary activities communicate and reinforce the company's performance standards. Each employee chooses how to respond to these messages about performance.
- Your objective is not to punish, but to change behavior.
- You are not the aggressor. The employee's choices about his or her behavior creates the need for discipline.
- Productive employees are discouraged when problem employees are ignored or tolerated.
- To ignore a poor performance situation is to be unfair to yourself and other employees who may have to pick up the slack created by an unproductive employee.

If we all think of discipline problems as genuine opportunities to foster development, we will correctly focus our energies on communicating effectively about performance.

Chapter Nine

The Art of Delegating

You've heard this before: "If you want something done, ask the busiest woman you know. She'll find time to do it." There may be a grain of truth in this, but it is not what being a manager is all about.

By now, you've successfully met some of your early challenges as a manager and you are gaining some confidence. Now is the time to remind yourself to delegate. "What?" you respond. "Now that I'm finally getting the hang of this managing business, I'm supposed to start giving it up?"

Well, yes. Managing means achieving the organization's goals by working through others. The only way this is going to happen is through effective delegation: the entrusting of your responsibilities and authority to others. Your goal is to build your workers' capabilities to manage and direct their own work. By empowering them, you bring their best efforts to bear on the company's goals.

Delegation is one of the principles of supervision that lie at the heart of the Performance Improvement Model (see page 30). It merits another brief look because, by now, you may be struggling to learn to let go of your new responsibilities. This is normal.

It is very tempting to slip into the supermanager persona. The supermanager does not delegate because he/she knows all, sees all, and pushes all the buttons to make things happen. He/she thinks of him/herself as some kind of reluctant superhero, upon whom everyone depends and upon whom the future of the company rests. His or her desk is the command center for everything that happens. No one does anything without letting the supermanager know first. He or she alone signs all paperwork. No decision is too small for the supermanager's attention.

Eventually, this approach breaks down. The organization continues to load the supermanager up with more and more responsibility (since he or she is so capable!) until, like crashing dominos, all of the jobs and tasks and commitments end up burying him or her.

This is one career-stopping crisis you can avoid. In particular, if you are applying what you know about planning and organizing, you can begin learning to let go on projects and assignments with low risk. It's important to practice this skill now, before you develop work patterns that will trap you into doing more than you are able.

If everyone above and below you on the organization chart perceives you as a manager who cannot or will not delegate, you will create flawed systems that are almost always self-defeating. And guess what—no one will ever give you the kudos you think you deserve. Those around you are more likely to say, "So what that you single-handedly did all this work." They will not thank you for closing them out of the process. Information, responsibility, and authority are the coins of the corporate realm, and if you do not share them by delegating them, if you do not empower others through delegation, you risk being surrounded by a work team that has no concern or investment in the outcome of your efforts.

And who can blame workers for resenting a manager who uses his or her position to disenfranchise them from their work? They care about the company's success, too, because they think of it as their personal success. Put that energy to positive use for you by delegating as much as you are able.

The high costs of failing to delegate do not stop with you. If you become too busy doing, instead of managing, the important work of planning, organizing, influencing, and facilitating does not get done. Instead of thinking about your department or work team one month or one year down the road, your outlook horizon shrinks to a few days or a few hours.

You were promoted to the managerial ranks because you worked hard and knew how to get the work done. You still need to work hard, but you must master new ways of getting the work done. Your old work patterns may have gotten you this job as manager, but they won't help you keep it.

To review: when you delegate, you confer your authority to make certain decisions to a person willing to accept the short-term responsibility for completing a task. Because they have a portion of your authority, they can act and fulfill their responsibility.

The integrity of the delegation process is protected by accountabilities transferred to your representative with the authority and responsibility. Should they fail to perform, they will be held accountable and will suffer predictable negative consequences.

Delegation is more than just handing off a job and walking away; Robert B. Nelson, author of *Delegation: The Power of Letting Go*, says it requires four steps:

Prepare to delegate.   You must select the right person to assign this responsibility to, and then you must mentally prepare to let go of any emotional investment you have in this responsibility. If you can successfully force yourself to disengage from the task you are delegating, you will stay out of the way and let your representative do the job while you move on to other tasks only you can do.

Delegate.   You need to seek agreement with your representative about the goals, performance expectations, level of authority, support of other team members, and positive and negative consequences for good or poor performance.

Monitor the delegation.   You must stay in touch with your representative in order to provide feedback. You play a critical coaching role here.

Evaluate the delegation.   How did each of you perform during this activity? Was it a win-win situation, or was someone disappointed? Would both of you do this again?

Following are a series of provocative questions intended to stir your self-assessment of your delegation practices. Are you doing it? Do you care to do it? Do you know what you don't know about being an effective delegator? You will probably find it useful to discuss these with another manager who has already mastered the art of delegation.

1. If your supervisor tells you that the organization is centralized, what can you assume about the decision-making process? How many decisions and what kinds of decisions can you delegate effectively?

2. Personally, what is your strongest base of personal power within the informal organization? Are you able to let go of the responsibilities and authority you have earned relative to your personal power?

3. What types of decisions, problems, and questions do you direct to your supervisor? Your colleagues? A technical expert? Which ones do you hold onto because you think you are the best one, or only one, to handle them?

4. How much time do you spend in conversations that delegate? Are you an effective delegator? Do your workers enthusiastically accept the work opportunities you present to them?

5. If you accept the responsibility for an assignment, but your supervisor withholds the authority, what are your chances for success? Do you practice this same habit with your workers?

6. Are you personally comfortable with the notion of letting go? What can you and your workers do to build the team's capacity and capability for delegation?

7. Do you like to have tasks delegated to you? Why? Under what circumstances are you most successful with the tasks delegated to you? Are you delegating to your workers in the manner in which you like to be delegated to?

8. Organizations are getting more complex, often causing employees to report to several supervisors concurrently. It can be argued that this actually diminishes an individual manager's control over any one employee. How does this new type of matrix organization affect the way you delegate?

9. Describe an organization you are familiar with that can be described as running smoothly. What makes this possible?

10. Describe an organization you are familiar with that is not operating well. How do you know it is having problems, and what would you recommend to remedy the situation?

You must learn to delegate. Delegation will allow you to rise above the limitations of your personal time and ability. By letting go of tasks that can be and should be done more efficiently by others, you put everyone's talents to better use.

Chapter Ten

The Art of Networking

If information is power (and it is), much of your influence depends on what you know and when you know it. You may not share the positional power of those at the top of the corporate hierarchy, but you can certainly make an important difference by mastering information about the day-to-day operations of the company.

Networking is commonly used to describe the process of giving and receiving business information via informal communication channels. Developing your information channels or network is a way for you to:

Learn what changes lie ahead.

Identify problems early.

Test and presell your ideas.

Defuse potentially damaging or embarrassing situations.

Make time work for you.

Give and receive off-the-record feedback.

Learn first-hand who is and is not doing his or her job.

Suggest and solicit ideas to improve operations.

Scout future job opportunities.

The following suggestions will help you recognize and make the most of networking opportunities.

HOW DO YOU GET PEOPLE TO TALK TO YOU?

Information is not going to flow to you automatically without some effort on your part. No one is going to pick up the phone and go out of his or her way to talk to you unless they sense that it is somehow in their best interests to do so. This means you have to earn their confidence and trust. If the people around you believe you to be fair and honorable, they will be more likely to confide in you.

Your position puts you on display. More people than you know are watching you. Does your "walk match your talk?" Do you keep your promises? Are you someone to be counted on? Can you hold your position, or do you just say whatever your listener wants to hear? You have to lay some groundwork to build the kind of communication network you want. Consider whether you are making it easy for people to share their thoughts with you by assessing your traits.

Are you a good listener? Are you ready to be quiet and let someone else talk? Some new managers become so full of their own ideas and concerns that they unintentionally shut others out. The people around you know when you are not really listening; you may be surprised with the thoughtfulness of their comments.

Are you accessible? People can't talk to you if they can't find you. If you intentionally keep a low profile in the plant or bury yourself in meetings, you are sending a clear nonverbal message that you are just too busy to listen. Go where your people are: in the plant, in the lab, or on the road. Don't be surprised if some important information comes your way via a casual walk down the hallway with someone who just happened to be going your direction. You don't have to be at every meeting, either. If you send a clear signal that you are accessible and you value your people's input, they will find their own way to communicate with you. You can send such a signal by holding brown bag lunches on every other Thursday, traveling with your technicians at least once a month, making a big deal out of implementing an employee's suggestion, starting each day with a walk through the plant, or something similar. Become an easy target for ideas and feedback. Don't give them an excuse for not speaking up.

Are you approachable? Does your style encourage people to open up to talk and listen? Or are your people starting to call you "ol' stoney face" or "dragon lady" behind your back? Few of your employees probably feel comfortable making a formal complaint or speech to the boss; make it obvious to them that you are receptive to conversation around the coffee pot, notes written on napkins, or whatever else makes them feel comfortable.

Are you trustworthy? This is basic. Can you keep your employees' confidences? Do you exercise discretion? Are you known for your common sense or your loose lips? Your employees take a risk when they talk to you, and your peers and bosses take a similar risk when they include you in discussions. How do you handle the information people share with you? Sure, you may have been trustworthy in the past, but will you be in your new position? It is common for new managers to misuse information because they are struggling to cope with new pressures. If you begin to use information to impress others, for example, you can be sure people will think twice before they share with you.

Are you fair? You may believe you are as fair as you always have been, but your view may not jibe with the perceptions of others. You have to manage how you are perceived. Do you appear to be playing favorites? Give even-handed feedback about performance? Misappropriate the ideas of others? Say or do things that can be interpreted as hypocritical or unethical? Be careful to be fair and look fair, even if it means taking a little extra time to overcommunicate; once judged as unfair, you will not have the luxury of frank and open appraisal to counteract this perception.

Are you dependable? What is your reputation for standing behind your commitments? For following through? For keeping your promises? If you're known for your consistency and predictability, your information network will have consistency, predictability, and integrity.

HOW DO YOU GET PEOPLE TO TELL YOU BAD NEWS BEFORE IT'S TOO LATE TO DO SOMETHING ABOUT IT?

What you hear from your information sources depends on your history of responses. They will predict your response to bad news based on their prior experience with you. Blame, shouting, recriminations, passing the buck, defensiveness, and similar responses are going to discourage the sharing of bad news. If this is what you really want—to never hear the bad news—then you are missing any opportunity to correct a bad situation before it gets out of hand.

The smart manager creates a supportive environment that encourages and rewards people who speak up when they see a problem. Isn't this why you're a manager in the first place—to solve problems and improve the quality of everyone's worklife?

Here are some of the steps you can take to foster an environment where people are not afraid to tell you bad news.

Be constructive.   Make it clear to the messenger with bad news that you are genuinely interested in understanding all the details and getting to work on a solution. The messenger will not suffer in your department.

Keep everyone informed and involved.   Demonstrate respect and confidence in your employees by sharing, not hoarding, information. The people you work with want and deserve information that affects them. Well-informed employees are generally more optimistic in their outlook and more resourceful, and therefore more helpful in problem solving. If you routinely share good news and bad news with them, they will do likewise with you. You will get as much and as good information as you give.

Express interest in them as individuals.   Get involved with their careers. What do they really like and dislike about their jobs? What are their dreams and passions? What do they think they do really well? When you add a genuinely personal element to your relationship with your employees, they are more likely to do likewise. If they are confident you are looking out for their interests, they will be much more likely to say, "Listen, boss, there's something you ought to know about that last shipment. . . ."

Use the information you receive responsibly. Do not underestimate the power of the grapevine. Others probably know more than you think, and if you misuse the information they already know from elsewhere, your information network will judge you as incompetent (you don't understand), irresponsible (you are a loose cannon, saying things to people without regard for the consequences), or unethical (you cannot be trusted).

Provide more than one or two communication channels. Since not everyone is comfortable making a presentation at a staff meeting, writing a memo, scheduling a one-on-one discussion with you, or confronting a problem head-on, you can help your network by making it clear you are receptive to information from everyone at anytime and in any manner they feel comfortable with. You may even want to use a suggestion box, questionnaire, or similar device so you don't miss anonymous sources.

Do something with the information you receive. Some information begs to be attended to. If someone shares a bit of crucial information with you, perhaps with great personal anxiety and risk, you owe it to your source to tell him or her what you are going to do with the information. Then, be sure you do it, perhaps even following up later. It is perfectly acceptable to do nothing except think about information you receive—in fact, sometimes that is exactly the right response—but you have to be straightforward about it with your source. "Bob, thanks for telling me about this problem. I had no idea it was this serious, and I know this was not easy for you. Let me tell you that I'm just going to sit on this for now, but I may need to discuss it with Mr. Foster next month. Of course, I will respect your confidentiality, and I will let you know what happens."

RATE YOUR NETWORKING SUCCESS

How do you know when your network is working for you? Here are some clues:

- You receive few surprises, either good or bad, because you know about most events before they occur.
- Your employees express support and follow through with constructive suggestions when problems need to be solved.
- You are among the first, not the last, to receive bad news.
- Your advice is routinely sought.
- Your sphere of contacts seems to be steadily growing.
- More people are sharing more information with you.
- You learn about future job opportunities early enough to act on them.

You know your network is in trouble when:

- You are being surprised by good and bad news; you seem to be the last to know of significant events.
- You detect a decline in information flow.
- Morale deteriorates.
- Warning signs come in the form of nonverbal actions (e.g., being left out of meetings, being "forgotten" when copies of reports and memos are distributed).
- Customer complaints increase (both outside and internal customers, such as other departments).
- Changes occur in employee behaviors.
- You notice a reluctance in people to volunteer information.
- You cease to receive positive or negative feedback about your own performance.
- You rarely hear about job opportunities or learn about them too late.

Take care of your information network, and it will take care of you!

Chapter Eleven

Choosing and Keeping the Best People

Each of us can relate to Peggy, Randolph's supervisor. Randolph fooled her, plain and simple. With plenty of computer experience in the food distribution business and good reasons for switching jobs, he "looked very good on paper"—in other words, he had an impressive resume. He interviewed well, too; he seemed sincere and talked a lot about "partnering." Peggy was relieved to find such a capable applicant, so she made him an offer on the spot. He accepted the job and started the following Monday.

Within two weeks, Peggy began to suspect Randolph was going to be a problem. Here's what Peggy heard from Randolph's work team leader when she asked for some feedback about his work:

"Some of his work is pretty good, most is just OK. I just wish he got more done. Randy spends a lot of time talking to people. I guess that's good, isn't it? I suppose he's trying to learn as much as he can so he can do his job better. He seems like a heck of a nice guy. I really like him. I'm sure he'll be fine after he gets used to our way of doing things."

A small alarm bell began ringing in the back of Peggy's mind. She quietly asked others some more questions about Randolph's performance. She learned he did not work well with people from other departments, seemed preoccupied with gossip and office politics, seemed to have trouble following through with assignments, and generally appeared to lack the industry knowledge and skills one would expect to find in a person with his experience. But still, everyone liked him and thought he would eventually be a good worker.

Taken one at a time, none of these deficiencies or behavior problems would be enough to justify termination. Looked at together, however, they spelled Trouble for Peggy.

Peggy initiated the reference check she knew she should have done before making Randolph an offer. She had known at the time that she was taking a shortcut when she skipped this step, but she excused herself when she thought of how difficult it had become to get anything more than name, position, and dates of employment from reference checks. Besides, she was nearly desperate to fill the position, her recruitment advertising budget was exhausted, and she was just plain tired of interviewing.

She was not surprised to learn that the references were out of town, out of business, or otherwise unavailable when she called. If Randolph's resume was fiction, she would have a hard time proving it. She had a difficult decision to make—should she give him the benefit of the doubt and try to make this position work for him, or should she cut her losses, admit her mistake, and suffer the political and financial costs of starting the job search all over again?

She made her decision later that evening. On her way out, she passed Jim at his terminal. "Burning the oil tonight?" she asked.

"Actually, I spent so much time helping Randy today that I got behind on my work," Jim said. "I would think he'd know more than he does about that new SuperDuper software, but he said his last company didn't use it the same way we do. Oh, well—I can see my kid play ball next week, right?"

Randolph is conning us, Peggy decided, and he has to go. She realized how unfair and demoralizing it is to make good workers take up the slack for a poor performer. She had a feeling that Randy was doomed to be a marginal performer, doing just enough to stay in his job and never performing badly enough to be dismissed. In other words, he was dead-wood-in-training.

Peggy fired him the next day on the basis of his marginal performance. He complained that he was not being given enough time to learn on the job. Peggy cut the conversation short, saying simply that early feedback suggested a serious gap between his actual level of experience and her expectations. Since this meant a performance problem she was unwilling and unable to tolerate, it would be in the best interests of the company and Randolph if they part ways now.

During the next few weeks, as she went through yet another round of recruitment ads and interviews, Peggy reflected on some of the realities of employee turnover.

Turnover in a workforce is expensive.   The process of finding, selecting, hiring, and training a replacement for a worker is burdened by unavoidable costs. Besides the obvious expenses of recruitment ads, employment agency fees, and relocation costs, there are indirect costs like interviewing time, orientation costs, training, lost productivity, and mistakes. One major retailer estimates training costs for each new hire at $5,000. These costs continue to go up every year.

Some turnover is desirable, some is unavoidable. The good news is that new hires can serve as a continual source of new energy and new ideas, helping to keep the company fresh and vital. The trouble is, the people you want to leave usually don't, and the people you want to keep leave too soon. Those who stay, but shouldn't, demoralize others with poor attitudes and work habits. Those who leave take a sizable investment of the company's time and money and expertise with them. In any case, the higher the turnover, the higher the cost. Most industries regard a turnover rate of 5 to 10 percent as normal and healthy.

The rate of turnover is a useful measure of employee satisfaction and corporate vitality.   If people like their jobs, they stay; if they don't, they leave. The manager's challenge is to listen carefully to employee concerns and regularly reinforce the idea that employees' success is tied to the company's success. If the turnover rate is too high, it may be wise to conduct exit interviews just prior to each employee's departure. Ask the soon-to-be-ex-employee why he or she is leaving. Do all the employees leave for reasons beyond the company's control, for example, going back to school, the spouse has a better job in another state, etc.? Or do you detect any patterns, such as lack of recognition, subnormal pay, or abusive management that can be remedied?

Nearly one-quarter of all businesses have turnover rates higher than 20 percent per year. In some industries, such as retail, average turnover rate is as high as 80 percent. Some banks, insurance companies, and restaurants report turnover rates as high as 200 percent among nonmanagerial employees—and they consider this normal! Just imagine how expensive is it to run a company when only a very few customer service people have been on the job longer than six months? Again, higher turnover means higher costs.

To calculate your company's or department's turnover rate, divide the number of people hired during a 12-month period by the average number of total employees. For example, if a company has hired 20 people in the past year, and its head count averages 63 employees over the course of the year, the company's turnover is about 32 percent. Keep in mind that turnover usually describes replacement workers—those employees the company recruits and hires to replace employees who have left. If the turnover rate is to be a useful measurement of employee satisfaction, any expansion or downsizing of the workforce needs to be considered when the turnover is calculated.

What can a company do about high turnover? Well, some companies pay their people to stay. This is the somewhat cynical "golden handcuff" approach that creates a situation where the employee cannot afford to leave. Some car dealerships, for example, pay an extra $150 sales bonus to salespeople in three installments. The final payment comes more than two years after the sale, and the employee can only collect if he or she is still working for the dealership. At other companies, incentives are more traditional, such as retirement plans.

Financial incentives and similar strategies are company-wide policy decisions that are beyond the scope of most individual managers (unless you are the human resources manager, in which case solving this problem should be one of your top priorities).

Can you, as just one manager, do anything about high turnover? In fact, you can do a lot. Because you influence many details of an employee's day-to-day work experience, you can have a profound effect on the three functions that contribute to turnover—recruitment, selection, and retention. If you handle these functions well, your company will not need a policy that throws money at employees to stop them from walking out the exit doors!

RECRUITMENT

Good help is getting harder to find. Not only are there fewer people out there looking for work each year, but you've probably gotten fussier about who you hire, too. Peggy's experience with Randolph reminded her that "saving" a poorly qualified employee, however nice he or she might be, requires a lot of extra effort. Sometimes you may decide that an on-the-job training opportunity is your best way to fill a position, but at least you'll be prepared for the extra work this approach requires.

As a manager, you cannot expect good employees to just appear when you need them. The personnel department is the traditional gatekeeper. It has the tough job of drumming up potential candidates for some jobs, while at the same time turning away many others.

Most personnel departments do a poor job, say personnel managers.

Theoretically, every time a job comes up, the personnel department casts a wide net, objectively evaluates everyone who indicates an interest in the position, recommends the top few candidates for interviews, and the company ends up with the best possible match between candidate and job description. That rarely happens in an efficient or consistent way, personnel experts admit. The selection process is much less objective and much less organized. Because there isn't enough time or staff, the personnel department is frequently buried in paperwork and unfulfilled requests and unreturned phone calls. The staff-up and ratchet-down cycles in some industries are so frequent and dramatic that personnel staffing levels rarely match the flow of paper. It's not surprising that the process occasionally deteriorates into barely controlled chaos.

It's more likely that someone in the screening process makes a quick decision about a candidate based on his or her work load that day, the size of the mailbag, the sound of the person's voice on the phone, the persistence of the caller, or the color of the paper on which the resume is printed. The personnel staffer may actually be in a "siege" mentality, so some decisions are made for the sake of expedience.

You can expect roughly 20 percent of your workers to be excellent employees, 30 percent to be marginal to disastrous, and 50 percent or so to be adequate to good. The haphazard recruitment/screening process just described will identify the excellent and the very worst. It will not, however, treat the middle group consistently. The result is that potentially good and very good employees slip through the cracks, causing the company to continue to pay high recruiting expenses to attract potential candidates. Just for fun, rummage through the "No" and "Destroy" bins and baskets in your personnel office to see the people you won't get a chance to consider.

Granted, the personnel professional knows the phone call and resume game better than you do. A lot of books and resume services advise the job seeker how to look and sound especially attractive. The job-seekers' deceptions are masked with gimmicks, so it is an ongoing challenge for the personnel staff to recognize the qualified.

It is in your best interests, and the best interests of the company, for you to become an active participant in the recruitment process. Be prepared to help in the recruitment process by providing whatever insights you can into the job or the hypothetical ideal applicant.

True story: A department manager at a printing company in the Midwest needed an electronic prepress operator. The manager intuitively knew there were ample candidates available, so he was puzzled when no qualified applicants were forthcoming from the personnel department. "You've got to get me a couple of *good* operators to look at," he soon complained to the staffing clerk.

"You get what we get," was the reply. "You should be grateful you have anyone to consider at all because the market is tight right now."

Upon further investigation, the manager learned that the recruitment ad was incorrectly run in the newspaper's "computer operators" category instead of the "printing" category. "I want a printing person who knows computers, not a computer person who may or may not know the printing industry," he explained.

This was a surprise to the personnel office's staffing person, who said, "Look at your job description—this person has to walk and talk like a computer nerd, nothing more. You don't say anything here about understanding inks, plates, or presses. If you wanted an artist, you should have asked for one."

A little more discussion yielded a better ad. It also gave the manager an opportunity to tell the staffing person where the potential applicants may be looking for work. In the end, the best applicants came from a nearby town in which the staffing person had not even planned to run an ad. However, the manager knew a large competitor in that town was restructuring his comparable prepress department. Were there likely to be some people laid off, or at least some people who were unhappy with the new structure? Sure. With the additional help of a newsletter that went to a computer users group, the manager had almost a dozen good candidates from which to make his selection.

The point of this story is that you need to communicate your personnel needs clearly and early to those involved in the hiring process. Find out what the routine is to process new hire requests at your company. Even an informal process, say, where you place your own classified ads and schedule your own interviews, requires that you familiarize yourself with the details. What does the company offer to new hires? Why should an applicant choose to work for your company? Who makes your final hiring decisions? Who else needs to interview final candidates? Who makes compensation decisions, such as how much to offer and when is an offer made? Make your hiring need everyone's priority. It is very helpful to your company recruiter if you can provide some suggestions about who the ideal candidate is, where he or she is likely to be working now, and how much of your budget you're prepared to spend to find this person.

You have to appreciate how much recruitment costs. It costs your company significant amounts of money to generate those applicants for you to interview, so treat every one as a precious opportunity. Consider:

> The average cost per hire for exempt job categories in 1992 rose 22.5 percent to $6,654, according to the Employment Management Association. This figure reflects direct, out-of-pocket expenses only. The additional indirect costs—interviewing time, lost productivity, mistakes and make-goods, training—vary for each company.

> The average cost per hire for nonexempt job categories in 1992 was $1,283, down one-third from the previous year.

> The average overall cost per hire in 1992 rose 22.5 percent to $4,207.

> The average cost to relocate a homeowner is about $40,000. The average cost to relocate someone who is renting is about $10,000.

The health of the local economy is the single greatest factor that affects your company's recruitment costs. The quantity of people looking for work in your community, as far as you're concerned, is directly related to the amount of effort and expense your company expends to fill your job requisition order.

If many people are out of work, for example, you may attract several hundred applicants for a single position with a simple, inexpensive ad you run in the Sunday classified section. If unemployment is low, you may have to run numerous ads, and then do even more, to attract the attention of even a handful of applicants. You may have to be very aggressive (i.e., uses a headhunter or employment agency to lure employees away from your competition, or recruit from another community) or very creative (i.e., pay bonuses for referrals, host a job fair or open house, or run radio or TV recruitment ads) to get even a few qualified applicants to look at your position.

After the quantity of available applicants, the quality of candidates you wish to interview is the greatest variable in recruitment costs. The more particular you are, the more you pay. A shipping clerk is easier to find and attract than an operator for a specialized piece of machinery.

Some experts are predicting a crippling shortage of qualified applicants by the end of this decade. Other experts say the predicted shortages are overstated because labor shortages are largely determined by local economies and local market conditions. Individual managers need only be aware that several trends are converging in ways never seen before. It is very likely that these trends will combine to have some profound effects on recruitment of qualified employees. Each employer speculates about the effects of the following trends:

- The birth rate is declining.
- The number of potential workers in the 18- to 24-year-old age group has been declining since 1981, creating an applicant gap of 4 million of these young workers that has since been filled by women and minorities. (During the 1990s, about 20 million new jobs are expected to be created in the United States. For the first half of the decade, the number of 18- to 24-year-olds available will be about 500,000 less than in 1980.)
- Our public education system is failing to teach enough people fundamental math and literacy skills. (The National Alliance of Business estimates that one million high school students drop out every year and that one in eight 17-year-olds is functionally illiterate.)
- The age of the average worker is rising.
- Specialists who straddle several areas of expertise (such as the prepress operator described above) lack training and training opportunities.

- Technology continues to change at a rapid pace.
- We are unprepared as a country to compete globally (only a small percentage of our workers can speak even a smattering of a second language).

Applicant shortages are showing up already in some sectors, such as health care, insurance, data entry, clerical, and secretarial. What's common about these jobs? They all require increasingly advanced levels of skill, such as a knowledge of office automation technology.

Three-fourths of American Management Association members recently surveyed expect problems in the future finding employees with needed skills. Employee shortages are already reported by 55 percent. Forty-four percent believe the anticipated labor shortage will increase their costs for orientation and training. Seventy-three percent say their companies have not developed any plans to hold on to their most-needed employees.

So where do you find the really good people? If the position is important enough, such as the skilled printing worker described above, you have to be prepared to try more than just the conventional methods.

There are some suggestions listed on page 184 that you can make to your personnel department to stimulate their thinking. Or, bypass the personnel department. Some of these techniques cannot be used effectively by personnel departments, so try to use them yourself. The chart includes representative cost-per-hire data for an "average" technical worker in an "average" industry:

Recruiting costs increase as more applicants are recruited. The least-costly source of applicants is the company's file drawer of resumes and applications previously submitted. As soon as the decision is made to advertise the job, costs begin to climb.

Recruiting costs also increase as higher quality applicants are sought. Walk-in applicants are available at no cost, but the quality is inconsistent. Typically, walk-in applicants are either the very best or the very worst.

You may or may not be the person who actually executes these techniques in your company, but either way, you should

Recruiting Source	Number of Responses	Sample Cost for this Source ($)	Cost per Response ($)	Number of Qualified Applicants	Cost per Qualified Applicant ($)
applicants on file	10	0	0	1	0
"walk-ins" with sign out front	5	0	0	1	0
internal job posting	5	100	20	1	100
weekly newspaper ad	25	2,000	80	4	500
Sunday newspaper ad	150	6,750	45	6	1,125
regional TV ad with 800 # line	700	10,500	15	10	1,050
local radio ad with 24-hour interactive phone tapes, fax line	35	1,155	33	2	577.50
employee/network referrals (with bonus)	10	500	50	3	167.66
trade magazine ad	12	1,320	110	4	330
state job service	6	0	0	1	0
your own job fair at hotel	17	2,500	147	5	500
industry job fair booth	80	8,000	100	5	1,600
public relations, i.e. "new product" announcement	6	540	90	1	540
employment agency with fee	3	9,000	3,000	3	3,000
bilingual direct mail to 5,000-name newsletter list	50	2,500	50	10	250

be aware of them. They each carry a price tag. You probably would never use all of these strategies, at least at the same time, but each has a place in your recruitment media mix.

The trade-off between quantity versus quality is clearly represented in the data above. It's not a numbers game, it's a percentage game. Over time, if you keep track of where you get your best results, you will become familiar with those sources that are worth paying for because they consistently deliver the best applicants—those to whom you ultimately end up making an offer. Interestingly, newspaper recruitment advertising and employment agencies together represent 75 percent of employers' total recruitment expenditures, yet these sources produce only about 45 percent of the new hires.

Three sources—personal networks, hiring from within the company via job postings, and referrals from other employees—consistently show up as the best sources for good employees who stay on the job for a long time.

After spending the money to get the responses in the first place, don't waste the money with a slow or cumbersome process of follow through. As soon as the personnel staff person has done an initial screening and presents you with a stack of resumes or applications, respond to them today.

Keep the process simple. You and the respondent want the same thing—just enough information to decide whether this relationship is worth pursuing. If it isn't, you both need to get to the point of saying, "Thanks, but no thanks," as soon as possible and in a respectful way. If it does merit follow-through, move decisively.

Amazingly, some companies routinely keep prospective employees waiting six weeks before responding. This shabby treatment is degrading, and communicates the corporate "we really don't care" message. Is that how the company would treat a customer? Of course not. After six weeks, most people would give up on a resume to which they received no response, figuring that it had been discarded, disqualified, or lost by a disorganized or arrogant corporation.

Keep in mind that one of the indirect costs is the screening time required to separate the qualified applicants from respondents. A response is often an inquiry for more information. Once the respondent learns a little more about the job, such as the salary and location of the company, that may be the end of it. It's a good idea to do as much prescreening as possible because it reduces the amount of paperwork you'll have to sort through, but you have to plan to do it. Spending just 3 minutes each with 700 resumes equals 35 hours of someone's time.

Finally, don't neglect your current employees. Let them know you are looking for new people. If you are not going to hire replacements because the company is downsizing, tell them that, too. Involve your workers in the process, and they'll help you with feedback, suggestions, and even referrals.

SELECTION

Be careful.

An entire training industry, complete with newsletters, videos, and seminars, grew up in the 1980s in an attempt to sort out the minefield of employment law. You and your company can be sued even for saying the wrong things or asking the wrong questions in an interview. If you have hiring authority, insist that you get your company's latest, and legally defensible, guidelines.

You are on solid ground if you remember that everything in the selection process should somehow relate to evaluating the candidate's ability to perform the duties of the job. Prior experience is relevant, for example, but marital status, ethnic background, and disabilities are not.

Step 1: Conduct an Initial Screening

Immediately eliminate the obviously poor candidates. If they clearly don't have the education, experience, or technical expertise, inform them of this in a respectful way.

Then, as soon as you can, use the phone to screen out others. This is essentially a mini-interview that lets you get a sense of how the person communicates while getting some additional details about his or her background and goals. Essentially, you are asking the same 6 to 10 questions of everyone about the critical aspects of doing the job in order to decide whether or not this person should be invited in for an interview. The conversation should last less than 15 minutes; any longer than that and you may as well cover the rest of the information in an interview.

This telephone call saves time for you and the job seeker. For example, if you know that the person must be able to run a boiler, or must have a certain educational background, or possess certain core job skills, ask her on the phone whether she qualifies. Nothing else will matter if these criteria aren't met, so they are a good filter. This also lets you give the prospective employee a general overview of the job, location, and type of work, which may cause her to withdraw from consideration.

Keep screening on the phone until you have the number of applicants down to a manageable number to interview, perhaps three to five candidates. Call them back and invite them in for an interview.

Keep track of which respondents came from which sources and which sources are yielding the most promising applicants.

Step 2: Conduct a Detailed, Job-Related Interview

This meeting is held at the company's facility. It is an attempt by each of you to better evaluate the prospect of working together. The interview can be an enjoyable, worthwhile experience, or it can be aimless and inconclusive.

You are like the blind man trying to describe an elephant by feeling only its trunk. You will learn only as much about this person as he or she wants you to learn. You want specific data, preferably the truth, including the negative information that will make it easy to decide not to hire this person. The applicant wants to tell you only that his greatest weakness is "sometimes working too hard," and, "in my eagerness to accomplish meaningful goals efficiently, I sometimes may be less than tactful."

If you are like most managers, you will quickly get a "nose" for the negative. Partially to counterbalance the positive story you are getting from the applicant, partially in reaction to the long list of interviews you need to wade through, you look for even a small negative that will allow you to disqualify this person. This is particularly true when you are interviewing for a job that can be performed by several or more of the applicants.

Some managers and professional interviewers say they base their decisions almost entirely on appearance, punctuality, and connections.

Other interviewers look for the candidate who will say exactly the right thing. These managers are too quick to "fall in love" with a candidate. The applicant is sensitive to the manager's verbal and nonverbal cues. It's not surprising that the applicant says what the manager wants to hear. It's also not surprising that little of substance is learned in these types of interviews, and that the decisions they lead to are often disappointing.

Ideally, your interviews will be fair and packed with information for both of you. Strive to efficiently cover the essential information: Can the applicant perform well in this job, and is he or she possibly compatible with you and with the company? You do not need to take valuable time on personal opinions or stories (especially yours—be quiet and listen to the applicant). First interviews that last longer than about 45 minutes tend to be redundant.

Start the interview with a brief (about five minutes) explanation of the job. This gives the applicant a few minutes to settle into the interview. It also gives you an opportunity to observe his or her listening skills. (Does he remember what you told him about overtime? Does he speak to what you told him were your chief concerns?) Use this time to also explain the general process you are following for hiring for this position (how many interviews you will have, by what date you expect to make an offer to someone, drug and assessment tests that will be required, etc.).

The most important part of the interview focuses on questions relating to the skills, characteristics, and abilities required for successful performance on the job. These skills, characteristics, and abilities are often referred to as *dimensions* of the job requirements. Typical dimensions include the following:

Oral communication skills
Written communication skills
Creativity
Leadership
Tolerance for stress
Persuasiveness

Flexibility
Resourcefulness/problem solving
Initiative
Analytical ability
Judgment

Ask for specific examples of behavior that demonstrate the applicant's strengths and weaknesses relative to particular dimensions. As soon as the applicant realizes that you have a pattern of asking for details about the good and bad, he or she is more likely to drop any pretense. Relative to the dimension of resourcefulness, for example, you might ask the interviewee:

How did you finance your education?

Can you describe a problem that you have had to solve that required unusual resourcefulness?

How do you describe your process of solving problems?

What are the types of problems you find most difficult to solve?

To explore the dimension of judgment, you may ask an applicant:

Why did you select radio broadcasting as a major?

What is your assessment of the current business climate in our industry?

Why did you make the change from performing to producing?

Which of the new XYZ technologies do you prefer? Why?

If the applicant appears to have the technical competence to do the work, try to assess his or her cultural compatibility with your company and department. To do this, be honest about the types of people and situations he or she will have to deal with. Are his co-workers confrontive, blue-collar good ol' boys? Are they academic types who tend to be a bit pompous? Are the first six months going to be filled with grunt work? Does your company value tradition and routine over innovation and initiative? Was the last new idea suggested in 1963, or do people compete for the *inspiration du jour* award? You must make a realistic appraisal of how well a prospective employee will function, adapt, and enjoy him/herself working here. Of course, this is a judgment call that requires a lot of sensitivity so as to not run afoul of antidiscrimination laws.

Keep your personal feelings about a person in check. Positive feelings about a person are a good compass, but they don't supply the locomotion to get you where you want to go. It's tempting to hire a person with whom you have an instant rapport, or who is a splendid listener for your war stories, or who looks like your high school sweetheart, or whom you feel sorry for, or who seems like a lot of fun. Very soon, this person is going to have to do a tough job for you. Focus on the applicant's ability to perform the job. Can he or she do the work? Will he or she do the work? Imagine, also, what it would be like to supervise this person. Will you be able to have tough, good-news-bad-news conversations about performance with this person?

Do not make statements that create unsupportable or indefensible positions, such as, "We are committed to a very low turnover rate," or, "We never fire anyone without a good reason," or, "Jobs with this company tend to be for life." Statements like these imply limitations on the company's power to discharge employees.

Do not state or imply that the employee is being hired for a specific length of time unless you are certain of it, as would be the case with a 12-week internship, or a 3-month part-time assignment. It's best if you talk about compensation in terms of weekly or monthly amounts; to use an annual figure may be construed as an agreement for at least one year of employment. If any materials (letters, memos, etc.) refer to an annual salary, the following should be added: "The statement of an annual salary is not intended to imply that the company agrees to hire any employees for a one-year period. All company employees are employees-at-will." (References to employees-at-will do not apply Montana, which has abolished the legal concept of employment-at-will.)

Have all job applicants sign an application form (or statement) that states something like the following: "I understand and agree that, if hired, my employment is for no definite period and may, regardless of the date of payment of my wages or salary, be terminated at any time. I understand that no person is authorized to change any of the terms mentioned in this employment application form." This is the essence of the employment-at-will relationship between employers and employees.

Finally, do not make any references to "probationary" or "trial" periods of employment. Some courts have ruled that the use of such terms implies that once the employee has passed the probationary or trial period, he becomes a "regular" employee who cannot be discharged except for probable good cause.

Step 3: Conduct a Second In-Depth Interview

This is reserved for only the serious finalists for the position. A second interview is not always necessary but can be beneficial to confirm your impressions. Do you still feel as strongly about the person the second time, or were you or he/she just having a particularly good or bad day? You may want to include short discussions with the key people on the work team who will be working with this person, or other supervisors in the company who can add to your perspective.

Step 4: Check Background References for Your Top Candidates

This gets tougher and tougher. Some companies are cautious because they fear defamation lawsuits by ex-employees. Many companies find it simpler to reveal only that so-and-so worked for this time period and that he held such-and-such title. Conversations with supervisors are not always allowed.

The breakdown of the process of obtaining references hurts good employees and offers protective cover for bad employees. Still, the reference check is a powerful evaluation tool that remains one of the best predictors of future performance because work habits and other behaviors are likely to be repeated.

At this stage in your discussions with your top candidates, these references are much more important than simply confirming information you already have. You are interested in how well this person performed in their last position and the former supervisor's insights into the applicant's strengths and weaknesses. For these top few candidates, references are worth the extra effort it sometimes takes to obtain them.

Actually, there is little legal danger from lawsuits if proper procedures are followed. These procedures apply to you when you are asked to provide references, too, and so they bear mentioning.

- Provide references only if the former employee has been informed of the type of reference that will be given *and* has signed a release.

- If no release has been signed, inform the company asking for the reference that it must instruct the applicant to contact the personnel office and make arrangements to sign the release form.

- Require those requesting references to make their requests in writing. Do not give, nor expect to receive, oral references.

- All responses should be provided in writing only. Granted, all this writing slows down the hiring process, but for the top few candidates, it's worth the effort. Remember the high cost of turnover? This ensures you're hiring someone who can really do the job, not just interview well. Besides, you start the reference check process prior to the final interviews, so you still have some waiting time that can be put to good use in this way. Finally, fax machines can be used to speed up the process.

- All responses should be written by only one or two individuals authorized to do so. These people should be knowledgeable about employment law limitations, so they can interview the supervisor involved and write references that comply with privacy laws, yet meet the need for information. Company attorneys can assist with training.

The writers of references must be sure that their written references contain only factual information (no opinions, please) and are limited to the factual matters identified in the signed release form.

- The ex-employee's signed release form for employment references and other employment data, such as performance management reports, should be filed and maintained.

Step 5: Conduct the Final Interview and Make the Offer

Once you've decided on the best candidate, decide what the final compensation, benefit, and job description will be and make the offer. Be prepared to provide much more detailed information about your company—you are now "selling" the position to the applicant. Hopefully, by now, there will be few surprises for either of you.

As soon as the applicant accepts the offer, determine where will he or she work, what will be his/her starting date, and other pertinent information. The personnel staff person in your company will help you work through the checklist of paperwork and introductions necessary to bring the new person into the company.

Hire with care. You will soon learn that getting and keeping good employees is the least painful way to build a competent and productive employee base.

RETENTION

Okay, you've hired a fine employee. You are about to make a significant investment in the training and orientation of this person. While you are getting your new employee started, your competition also has hired its own choice of best applicants for a comparable position. Whoever does the better job of utilizing their person, and whoever manages to keep them longer, will receive the greater benefits.

How will you keep this new employee, and your other employees, working on your team? Doing them the favor of allowing them to keep their jobs isn't enough anymore! They are working for you in the context of the following factors.

- The educational qualifications of the most desirable workers are rising, but so are their expectations for tangible and intangible rewards from their work.

- The number and amount of bona fide benefits and opportunities you can offer is likely to plateau or even decline.

- The implied social contract between employee and employer has been rendered virtually meaningless in the last 15 years. Corporate loyalty is increasingly rare, and it doesn't happen without explicit efforts by the company. The employee believes that since the company's loyalty to him is only conditional, his loyalty to the company is equally and justifiably fickle.

- The proportion of jobs held by white, middle-class males is shrinking, according to different studies by the Institute for Educational Leadership and the Hay Group. About 83 percent of the new workers entering the workforce between now and the year 2000 will be either women, minorities, or immigrants. Many of these new workers will likely have different attitudes, expectations, needs, and skills than traditional companies are accustomed to. Integrating them into productive work teams may require substantial changes in traditional training and retention practices.

- The typical American family is no longer easy to define— there are an increasing number of single-parent families, dual-career families, and blended families due to divorce and remarriage. Again, this suggests that your workers, regardless of race or ethnic background, will have different priorities and needs. How will you respond when someone needs time away from work to deal with family issues like illness or court custody hearings? If your employee is a shift leader in your plant *and* a primary care giver at home, how much flexibility are you prepared to grant so he or she can juggle both sets of responsibilities? Other areas where diversity issues are likely to emerge are:
    1. Customer relations (Which languages will your repres‑ entatives speak? How will the disabled access your products, services, and employment opportunities?)

2. Technology (Are your employees coming to work with the necessary skills?)
3. Your corporate culture (What kind of company do you want to become? Do you really want to include or exclude certain groups of people? What are the implications of these decisions relative to recruitment costs, marketing efforts, etc.?)

Your new employee requires the same things as your current employees, only more: more training time, more career development time, more orientation time to the company's business and goals. Allow a realistic period of time for a new hire to become accustomed to and flourish in her new position by organizing her training in a logical sequence with performance benchmarks.

A production scheduler, for example, may need nine months of on-the-job experience before she is doing everything called for in the position's job description. You certainly cannot wait that long before deciding whether this person can do the job for which she was hired. On the contrary, you will take the job description apart, sequence it, and train her for it. Then, after two weeks, she will be able to process materials requests; after 30 days, she will schedule production for just one line and one shift. If she hits the benchmarks along the way, she'll probably end up knowing how to do the whole job by the end of her training time.

Training by itself doesn't hold employees, though. They need to be confident that their long-range personal goals are being met by their continuing employment. Are you, as their leader, spending enough time communicating the larger corporate vision? Are you clearly linking their career plans and objectives to those of the company? Are you listening to them for signs of confusing or frustration or disappointment? Through conscientious training and career development activities, your employees will know they are valued. Isn't that what we all need to know?

Finally, don't neglect the interpersonal side of your employees. Everyone wants to have friends at work who trust and respect them. Are your employees cultivating friendships with each other? Field technicians who are away from the office most of the time need to have more of a relationship with their co-workers than just a voice over the phone or radio, for instance. One field maintenance company schedules monthly meetings just so employees can spend "play" time together. What can you do to create a friendly environment for your workers?

To get and keep your best workers, you need to hire them based on the work they can do, not on how they look or how they live. Your most productive workforce may be a team knitted together of:

Traditional-looking workers with contemporary problems.

Temporary workers.

Foreign nationals.

Part-timers.

Job sharers.

Work-from-home workers.

Workers from merged or acquired companies.

The next chapter provides some more insights about working with a diverse workforce, which includes disabled workers.

Chapter Twelve

Managing a More Diverse Workforce

Are you hearing more talk around the water cooler about diversity? Are you hearing more racial slurs against co-workers? Discovering more anti-gay graffiti in the washroom? Seeing people get angry and confused when they talk to each other? Are you sensing that your work teams are becoming more cliquish, more isolated from each other, more divided into groups of those who are "in" and those who are "out"?

Like it or not, "difference" has become an issue at work. Rightly or wrongly, characteristics that used to be accepted or ignored are now defining our working relationships in obvious and sometimes disruptive ways.

As we discussed in the previous chapter, diversity among potential employees affects your recruitment efforts; as we'll see in this chapter, diversity amidst your current workforce also affects your management approach. We'll examine a workable two-part method for dealing with diversity in this chapter.

WHAT IS DIVERSITY, AND WHAT'S IT DOING AT WORK?

Diversity is differentness. By itself, it is a simple idea and a neutral term. Diversity becomes a problem when workers do not accept, understand, appreciate, or tolerate the differences between each other.

Of course, the workplace always has been a place where people of different colors and cultures met. It is in the workplace that the notion took root that America is a melting pot of different types of individuals, all setting aside their differences and contributing their best efforts to build something larger than themselves.

Diversity issues are us-versus-them problems. They are also called racism, sexism, elitism, prejudice, bigotry, bias, and a dozen other such terms. These in-group versus out-group issues have been with us a very long time. They have excluded, denied, demeaned, discriminated, and devalued qualified workers for shameful reasons. Thankfully, our society has continued to inch towards a vision of equal opportunity for everyone.

You may have experienced some of these diversity problems personally. At some level, you bring those experiences to work with you every day. So do your workers. The struggle to learn to work together despite our differences continues for each of us, in our own ways.

Traditionally, accepting a job meant accepting the organization's culture. If an employee wanted to be promoted, he had to fit in, so he or she worked hard to look and speak and act like his or her co-workers. This is called *assimilation.* To get along, people learned to go along: Blacks talked like whites, gays stayed in the closet, feminists quietly accepted the few jobs they were offered. This attitude frequently extended beyond the workplace: If everyone else on your shift joined the bowling team or played golf or went fishing or belonged to a club, you didn't mind changing yourself in order to assimilate.

In the good old days, long before you became a manager, these situations were not likely to be problems. The differences between the employees were still present, but the corporate culture was strong enough to smooth over most potential conflicts. Because they wanted and needed to keep their jobs, employees were motivated to avoid conflict and conform, even if that meant swallowing their pride, accepting unfairness, settling for less than they deserved, tolerating bigotry, and being deaf to the mean-spirited taunts of co-workers. In short, the power of assimilation made it unnecessary for a manager to solve problems rooted in diversity.

Now many more employees consider themselves empowered to control a greater part of their life at work. They value their own autonomy and authority. They want to feel personally effective. They want to make decisions and be held accountable for results. They are also ready to promote their own political and personal agendas. In short, they no longer step willingly into the mold presented by the corporation.

Fast forward to your company and your job in the here and now. How are you feeling these days about being assimilated?

> Aren't you less willing today to change yourself to fit the company's mold of the up-and-comer?

> Aren't you resisting the unwritten rules of behavior that traditionally led to the traditional definitions of success? (Some examples include arriving early, working late, sacrificing your kid's ball game for another meeting, never turning down an assignment or transfer, talking about sports, dressing just so, or driving an American car.)

> Aren't you just a little more realistic about trusting your company to provide you with job security from now until retirement?

You know more and more workers in your company who are thinking and feeling differently about how they fit in. These are times of "unassimilated differences." People are more comfortable with their differences now, and some are even prepared to defend them and advocate for them.

Managing diversity means dealing with new attitudes of empowerment, but it also means much more than that. Your management challenges relating to differentness are more than just shifts in your employees' attitudes. The basic makeup of your workforce has started to change in the last decade. Demographers, sociologists, and labor market experts who earn their living by tracking these statistics predict these changes will accelerate until we reach a new balance or blend of diversity sometime in the next century.

Consider just three of the fundamental changes in the makeup of your workforce that you will probably need to deal with. We looked at these as recruitment challenges in Chapter 11; as we'll see in this chapter, they are also management challenges.

- The proportion of jobs held by white, middle-class males is shrinking, according to different studies conducted by the Institute for Educational Leadership and the Hay Group. About 83 percent of the new workers entering the workforce between now and the year 2000 will be either women, minorities, or immigrants. Many of these new workers will likely have different attitudes, expectations, needs, and skills. Integrating them into productive work teams probably requires lots of changes in the old-fashioned, traditional company with which you are familiar.

- There are an increasing number of single-parent families, dual-career families, and blended families due to divorce and remarriage. Again, this suggests that your workers—regardless of their race or ethnic background—will have different priorities and needs. How will you respond when someone needs time away from work to deal with family issues like illness or court custody hearings? If your employee is a shift leader in your plant and a primary care giver at home, how much flexibility are you prepared to grant so he or she can juggle both sets of responsibilities?

- Finally, managers like you must commonly knit together a workforce of temporary workers, foreign nationals, part-timers, job sharers, stay-at-home workers, and workers from merged or acquired companies.

As noted in Chapter 11, the other areas where diversity issues are likely to emerge include the following:

- Customer relations (Which languages will your representatives speak? How will the disabled access your products, services, and employment opportunities?)

- Technology (Are your employees coming to work with the necessary skills?)

- Your corporate culture (What kind of company do you want to become? Do you really want to include or exclude certain groups of people? What are the implications of these decisions relative to recruitment costs, marketing efforts, etc.?)

Your workforce is getting more diverse every month, and your workers are dealing with their "differentness" from each other in new ways. Lucky you—you get to manage them! Welcome to the ranks of management, 1990s-style. One way or another, you have to manage your team of workers with different backgrounds, different levels of experience, different expectations, and different values to even higher levels of performance.

WHAT DOES IT MEAN TO MANAGE DIVERSITY?

No one really manages diversity. Diversity is simply a fact of life with which we have to deal. The best you can hope for is to manage amidst diversity.

In this chapter, we'll explore one workable two-part method to manage amidst diversity:

Part 1—Problems caused by diversity issues should be handled as performance problems.

Part 2—Solutions to diversity problems require more effective interpersonal communication skills.

Simply put, managing a diverse workforce means managing amidst unassimilated differences. Some people call this cross-cultural supervision. In spite of the differences between your workers, you must keep them focused on the overall performance of the organization. Effective cross-cultural communication about performance requires new kinds of interpersonal communication skills.

What do diversity problems look like?

Some are easy to see, like the Native American worker who does not want to give up his or her cultural or racial identity and the woman who does not want to give up her femininity, and yet each wants the same opportunity to be hired and promoted as any other qualified employee.

Some diversity problems are not so easy to see, such as the gap between older and younger managers. If the younger managers' values and notions of success are different from the older managers', there is a cultural difference that may

Managing Amidst Diversity

Managing Diversity Is	Managing Diversity Is NOT
. . . building systems and a culture that unite people in a common pursuit without undermining their diversity.	. . . another way to refer to just those groups of people protected by antidiscrimination laws. Diversity, in this sense, is a code word for equal employment opportunity (EEO) and affirmative action requirements. Diversity programs, then, are programs that extend and enhance these legally protective programs. This narrow view does not include other types of differences that have similar effects but lack legal status.
. . . taking differences into account while developing a cohesive whole.	. . . a litmus test for "political correctness." The "it's good for diversity" argument is often the justification for a broad, liberal social agenda that includes an "improved consciousness" regarding racism, sexism, and heterosexism. In this context, diversity programs are mechanisms to administratively impose certain ways of thinking and speaking about other people that are supposedly free of all potential bias and negative implications. For example, "physically challenged" is the politically correct way to describe the disabled. Generally, this interpretation of diversity has a negative effect: Excessive and contrived efforts to distinguish differences cause people to focus on that which keeps them apart, not that which brings them together.

lead to conflict. What happens when the older manager won't work late or the younger manager won't accept a transfer, for example?

Personality conflicts can be viewed as diversity problems, too, such as when "analytical" personality types have difficulty with "expressive" persons. In some circles, chronic differences erupt between those with different beliefs, whether about religion, politics, or visitors from outer space. Even the type of work a person does can be considered a potential source of diversity problems. Production workers don't always understand people who work with computers, accountants don't always appreciate marketers, and so on.

The questions that begin, "What do I do about . . .?" are the diversity issues facing you, your workers, and your company. They defy simple categorization because they are completely unique to your situation and circumstances. For some people, the issues will be cultural differences between races; for others, the issues will be between young and old managers. Some examples of potential diversity issues are listed in the table on the next page.

The broad view of diversity, and the one we use throughout this book, recognizes diversity in all its forms as a fact of life. Differences exist between people of different ages, backgrounds, experiences, and so on, in addition to the more obvious differences between races, cultures, and religions. Everybody is diverse.

Okay, diversity includes you, me, and everyone else. So what? Ah, this is the challenge, isn't it? Once we recognize our differences, what do we do about them?

As we noted before, at one time your company may have pretended to ignore differences between workers or used them as the basis for hiring, firing, and promotion decisions. That's not legal anymore.

Essentially, rather than ignoring diversity or resisting it, contemporary managers must find and use the potential benefits of diversity. They must value diversity, not just for its

Possible Differences That Define People	Can This Person Work. . .		. . .With This Person?
Morals	homosexual: "I feel so different from everyone else and I'm angry almost all the time."	versus	religious conservative: "God's plan is the only plan. Sinners be damned."
Values	older craft worker: "It's not right. Do it again. "	versus	younger craft worker in same dept.: "It meets the customer's specifications. Ship it."
Identity	Asian woman: "I will tell you exactly who I am before you ask."	versus	Asian man: "I keep my identity inside. It is private, very private."
Expectations	Native American computer programmer: "We're 100 years behind because of isolation and genocide. The white man owes me."	versus	Native American truck driver: "I always get what I want because I work hard for it. Everyone else should get ahead the same way."
Goals	Black male manager: "I'm here to get the job done and make a profit in the process."	versus	White female manager: "I'm here to make the world a better place, and that means building consensus and empowering people, as well as making a profit for the company."

own sake, but because diversity among workers can be a distinct competitive advantage and a generally positive influence. Ideally, a diverse workforce is more resourceful in making productivity gains, more responsive to customers, and more interesting to work with than its one-gender, one-culture competitors.

Let's look at the two components of one workable way to successfully managing amidst diversity.

PART 1: PROBLEMS CAUSED BY DIVERSITY ISSUES SHOULD BE HANDLED AS PERFORMANCE PROBLEMS

Diversity is a fact of corporate life. In the abstract, it is neither positive nor negative, neither a blessing nor a problem. It is neutral. You do not set out to do something about diversity without a focus.

Managing workers, however alike or dissimilar, is about achieving performance expectations and making a profit. Managing means reaching organizational goals, whether the workforce is diverse or not.

For most managers, diversity becomes an issue when it affects job performance. In an ideal world, you anticipate conflict before it arises, but this rarely happens. You likely will realize your need to address diversity only after performance begins to suffer because people cannot work together. This almost always starts as a negative incident between two employees who cannot reconcile the differences they perceive between each other.

With some effort on your part to raise their awareness of each other's viewpoint and the value of their respective contributions, a negative incident between two employees can be turned into a positive experience. Diversity becomes a positive influence when the work team utilizes the differences between its members to solve problems in new ways, relate to new types of customers, and so on.

Imagine if you abruptly discovered your diversity problem this way: You enter your office to find two of your punch press operators glowering at each other. One is white; he has worked for the company for 10 years. The other operator is younger, black, and only recently hired. They scuffled a few minutes earlier in front of the department bulletin board in the lunchroom. Your job is to get both of them back to work, but first you must diffuse this situation before someone gets hurt. You listen to each of them explain what happened, but finding fault and assigning blame is not the point—you need to resolve the larger issue between these two so this sort of thing doesn't happen again.

The older, white operator says: "I resent him, plain and simple. Just because he's black, he thinks he can come in here and run this place. I've been here longer. I don't think he should even be thinking about applying for the lead operator position."

The younger, black operator says: "I'm as qualified as he is. I just want my shot at the American dream. I'm not asking for any special treatment like he thinks I am. He just thinks equal treatment for *me* is somehow special treatment."

Is this a diversity issue? Sure. But it clearly has more complexity that just a black-versus-white racial problem. The two operators see each other as different in a number of ways—age, background, experiences, as well as the color of their skin. The white operator may be a racist; he may not be. He may be prejudiced, but not willing to admit it. The black operator may be overly aggressive, or he may not be.

From your perspective, it doesn't really matter. Your task is to get them both back to work, and the best way to do that is to get them to focus on the job at hand.

You decide to treat them both like adults. "Look, guys—I can't tell you how to think about each other or treat each other off the job, but here, on the job, we value your differences. Each of you brings something different to the party. I'm not talking about generalizations, like all black people think this way or that way, or all white people do this or that. I'm saying that I, and this company, value each of you as an individual contributor to our objectives.

"We all have to get back to work. That's the first rule. We have to find some way to work well together, safely and productively. That's the second rule. Rule 3 is if we can't find a way to follow rule 1 and rule 2, you can't work here."

You've set the stage for a resolution to this problem by making the company's expectations very clear. Your company does not tolerate behavior that has a negative effect on performance, period. Measured by this standard, all employees are equals. By linking employee behavior to job performance, you focus on narrow, observable changes while avoiding attempts to mandate politically correct attitude changes.

Some consultants specializing in diversity issues will suggest that the appropriate way to handle the above incident is to sensitize both employees to the cultural bias of the other. "Black people are like this," and "White people are like this," are the messages coming out of some diversity programs. Resist these well-intentioned, "feel-good" programs that simply use company time to swap one generalization for another. Generalizing about any group is wrong and counterproductive. It is ironic that some efforts to break down the barriers between people merely substitute one simplistic misunderstanding for another.

Your two quarreling employees need to get to know each other better. If they understand each other better, they are more likely to be more tolerant and understanding of each other. If their anger towards each other is rooted in generalized thinking about the other race, anything you can do to get them to personalize the problem will help. Generalizations are poor substitutes for independent thinking; give them a forum to talk with each other or a common goal to work towards and they are likely to get past their fuzzy ideas about each other. As their manager, you can make job security a good reason for them to try cooperation.

Practically speaking, however, your two employees probably already know each other well enough to know they dislike and distrust each other. They already have personalized their problem. Racism is probably buried somewhere within their relationship, but who knows?

Your best strategy is to frame this problem as a performance problem. Try saying something like this: "I don"t know *why* you can't work together. I can tell you that *what* you are doing, and not doing, is affecting the performance of this department. I am not your social worker or your therapist or your mother, so I can't do very much to help you work through your personality differences. I *am* your manager, though, and I can control the consequences of your behavior and poor performance.

"If you persist in making the shop floor your personal boxing ring, you'll both be fired. Consider yourselves warned for the first and only time.

"I am willing to provide a place and a time for you to work out your differences, but only if you both tell me you want to try. If you can live with your bad feelings for each other and still work together, fine. But if you want to make some effort to improve the situation, that's fine, too, and I'll buy the coffee. I care about both of you as valued employees, but I care about the overall performance of this department as well. Is that clear?"

PART 2: SOLUTIONS TO DIVERSITY PROBLEMS REQUIRE MORE EFFECTIVE INTERPERSONAL COMMUNICATION SKILLS

The other component to handling your diversity problems is better interpersonal communication.

In the example above, the manager efficiently and effectively dealt with a potentially explosive situation by focusing on the performance of the employees. Once again, this performance paradigm and the Performance Improvement Model provide a useful framework for setting priorities and making decisions.

But, successfully resolving this problem also required the manager to communicate with the employees in a very direct and personal manner. Successfully managing amidst diversity depends on your ability to communicate effectively like this often. So what if you correctly regard a problem as a performance problem, yet cannot help your employees see it the same way? Your thoughts about performance cannot become actions unless and until you speak up.

Think about the cultural differences between you and your employees when it appears that you are not being understood, for example. If you ask a member of your work team to do something, and he nods his head and says yes as if he agrees with you, but then he doesn't follow through, consider the possibility of miscommunication. He may have said yes to indicate he understood, but he may not have actually agreed with you. This reaction is more common in some cultures that regard verbal confrontation as disrespectful, but it could happen with anyone who is shy or confused, too.

Communication problems occur for lots of reasons. Some of the reasons are cultural; many more are simply a case of personal communication styles.

CONFUSION ABOUT DIVERSITY

Managing diverse workers is not about getting them to be nice to each other or to like each other, although these would be pleasant by-products. Your job is to create the environment that enables them to do their jobs. Usually this means doing some things within the performance paradigm that at least fosters mutual respect, such as making time for them to discuss their problems and hold team meetings. Let them address the details of their own interpersonal relationships by themselves, at their own pace.

Pay attention to the cues you receive from your human resources department for the company's official position and program offerings relative to diversity. In fact, not everyone believes job performance is an appropriate framework for dealing with diversity in the workforce.

Because the notion of a more diverse workforce has different implications for different people, many different and even conflicting meanings have crowded under the diversity umbrella. The diversity issue is a catch-all phrase used by several different constituencies in the organization. They each acknowledge the facts of diversity—it's always been here, and it's going to become more of a factor in the coming decades—but they do not always agree about what to do about it. Some people believe the company has a social responsibility to promote a socially progressive agenda.

At its worst, managing your diverse worker population may seem like one part therapy session, one part political science class, and one part babysitting club. This is because many workers are unable or unwilling to set aside their personal agendas or problems for the benefit of the work group's productivity.

A disabled client confided that she has become frustrated about the notion of diversity. "I used to feel just the opposite," she said. "I thought it was about time that the corporate consciousness got raised and the rest of us got a chance to do our thing. But now I get defensive when I hear, 'This is good for diversity.' I brace myself for a shrill, intolerant ideological argument, another narrow political agenda. Diversity is becoming a code word for political correctness. It's pushing us apart, not pulling us together."

If you are a white male, perhaps you have already heard that certain nicknames, attitudes, and practices are no longer acceptable because they offend or oppress someone. Perhaps you, or your group, or your company, has already been stung by an "-ist" accusation: sexist, racist, elitist. Perhaps you are wondering what happened to such a simple and fair-minded concept as mutual respect.

Perhaps you are a person of color, or disabled, or an older person, or a woman. For you, diversity may be an essential and long-overdue awakening of the collective corporate consciousness. Perhaps you, too, are wondering what happened to such a simple and fair-minded concept as mutual respect.

Diversity has become a buzzword, and it's probably suffering from a case of overexposure. Too many management consultants, sociologists, and politicians have used it to further their own agendas, hence the confusion and frustration about its application.

At the end of the day, it is your understanding and appreciation of the concept of diversity as it applies to your people that will make a difference. Don't make it more complicated than it needs to be, don't get trapped by those who are promoting a larger social agenda, and don't ignore your instinct and common sense that guide your interpersonal communications.

WHAT CAN I DO?

You have a lot of valuable experience working in your favor when it comes to managing a group of diverse workers. In fact, you may be ahead of your senior managers when it comes to understanding diversity. If you just recently came off the production line to assume the manager's role, all the better, because you know the diversity issue first hand.

You can lead your workers in their understanding of diversity problems. Tell them diversity issues are business issues, not moral issues. Tell them problems with differences between people cost the company money. Tell them diversity is about attaining better performance via better interpersonal communication. Tell them they need to communicate *more* with each other, even if they risk making a few mistakes and unintentionally offending someone.

Your objective is to build a team of heterogeneous workers that function as productively as homogeneous workers. Ideally, you will tap into a reservoir of new talents that will make your new, increasingly diverse culture even better than it was before.

What more can you do beyond setting a leader's example? Following are a few suggestions.

Educate yourself by studying diversity issues via books, videotapes, and programs. Better still, talk with workers who seem to be struggling with it. When you can put a personal story behind a situation, you are more likely to learn from it and teach it to others.

Raise the profile of the diverse nature of your work group by talking about it candidly. Do this in the spirit of mutual respect for individuals and within the context of improving the performance of the overall organization. If you are uncomfortable facilitating a discussion like this, ask for help from your human resources department or an outside communications consultant.

Participate in making sure that your company is in compliance with the Americans with Disabilities Act of 1990. Checking your policies and measuring your doorways, for example, can be a personally enlightening experience, plus it sends a clear, positive message about your intentions.

Chapter Thirteen

Troubleshooting Performance Problems

Management is not a science. It is an imprecise art, applied to people and events that are uncontrollable and unpredictable. The goal of management is not to simply minimize problems or inefficiencies; it is to lead the organization forward in spite of problems and inefficiencies.

Imagine that you are a facilities manager and your department has been assigned to implement a new toxic substance control system. This is an important project that can help the company protect the environment while lowering the costs of future liabilities. It is clearly a high-priority project with extra visibility to boost your career. Even though you may take extra time to plan, staff, motivate, and monitor this project, you know your work may be set back by any of the following:

New information from inside or outside the company.

People failing to do what they promised to do.

People doing less than they committed to, or doing their work differently than you expected.

Schedule or budget limitations imposed on you by someone else.

Other corporate priorities that conflict.

It's unrealistic to expect yourself to anticipate every factor affecting every employee and to manage so no problems occur. Business management, and life, for that matter, are just not that simple. Sooner or later, as you set about to achieve your group's objectives by planning, organizing, influencing, facilitating the work of others, and communicating about performance, people problems will crop up.

This chapter offers some examples of situations you may find troublesome. Some of these problems require you to act immediately, such as those affecting safety, discipline, budgeting, and scheduling. Other problems, like inadequate training, low morale, and poor communication, sneak up on you over a long period of time, bleeding the organization's profits because of bad habits left unchallenged too long.

The suggested remedies apply the principles of supervision, the four functions of management, and key performance communication skills. These are useful frames of reference to get you started on solutions to similar problems of your own.

This chapter also includes general guidelines about discipline and termination to help you approach problem situations in a logical, fair, and legally defensible manner.

Before we look at prescriptions for specific types of problems, let's look at an approach that works when troubleshooting most types of problems.

TURNING COMMON SENSE INTO COMMON PRACTICE

Your common sense and good judgment are two of your best problem-solving tools. Think about what you already know about the problems you have to troubleshoot as a manager. They share characteristics with which you are well acquainted.

Poor performance. Most problems are manageable when viewed as performance problems instead of personality problems. You have at least some influence and control over the behaviors and measurable results of your workers; you cannot affect their attitudes or thoughts.

Poor communication about performance. Misunderstandings are inevitable when people are not communicating clearly or completely. Co-workers need effective communication to understand what and how to do their jobs. Not everyone has to agree with everyone else, but they do have to understand each other.

Conflicting or confusing expectations. When people don't know what is expected of them, they become insecure and defensive about their actions. Most people genuinely want to meet the expectations of those around them—as soon as they can discover what those expectations are! When performance expectations are met, most problems go away or find their own solutions.

Conflicting or confusing priorities or processes. If your workers are unclear about the organization's priorities or processes, they will make incorrect decisions they may later regret. After repeating what they perceive as errors, they may cease to contribute by delegating upwards or deferring their responsibilities to others. This fosters employees' dependence on you, making them reluctant to decide or act without getting your approval. In turn, this situation can cause an organization to stagnate and shun new ideas.

Surprises. No one likes surprises, including your employees. Their experience has taught them that most surprises are unpleasant, such as unwanted transfers, layoffs, bad reports, and complaints. If they have not been forewarned and given time to prepare, you can presume you have taken one big step away from a solution. There are lots of ways to signal to people that you are unsatisfied with their performance; your challenge is to find the one that gets the message understood clearly and quickly.

I call these basic problems the *frustrating five* because one or more of them always seem to be present when there is a performance problem. They wear a hundred different masks in the workplace, but you will recognize them when you look below the surface of a problem situation. Do your employees feel alienated? Angry? Defensive? Reluctant to risk participating? Are they acting out their feelings at your expense? How many of your management problems are rooted in one or more of the frustrating five?

Common sense suggests that everything you can do to remedy the frustrating five is highly beneficial. Focus on the measurable performance issues first. Take time to give feedback about performance. Clarify expectations and priorities whenever they change. Avoid surprises.

Common sense is often uncommon practice, however. To uncover the frustrating five and develop a remedy to these common ills, I suggest you approach each problem by first answering the following sequence of questions:

1. *Whose problem is this?* If I can do something to affect the solution, it's at least partially my problem.

2. *How does this problem affect performance?* If it doesn't, perhaps I shouldn't let myself be distracted by it.

3. *Are performance expectations clearly understood by everyone?* If not, why not? Sooner or later, the differences have to be discussed.

4. *Is it clear how this performance contributes to the organization's priorities?* Explain what is important to the organization and why.

5. *What commitments have been made?* Business communication is a cycle of requests and promises.

6. *What is the gap between expected and actual performance?* Does everyone understand my description of the problem?

7. *What are each person's suggestions for solving this problem?* Get everyone involved and committed to a resolution.

8. *What have we decided to do?* Talk is not enough; a clear decision is the best protection against the reappearance of this problem.

Pretty basic stuff, right? Using common sense, fairness, clear communication, and mutual respect, let's look at approaches to the following problems that affect performance.

PROBLEMS THAT AFFECT PERFORMANCE

Problems Between People

Problem: *Failure to live up to commitments.*

Situation: You like Scott as a person, but he's driving you crazy because he makes and breaks commitments so casually. How can you persuade him to follow through on his share of agreements?

Suggestions: Scott likes to please people, so he is quick to say what he thinks you want to hear. He may not understand how displeased you are when he plays fast and loose with commitments. To take four steps forward:

- Express your frustration and disappointment each time he lets you down.
- Express your pleasure when he follows through as you both agreed.
- Structure your conversations so they make all requests and promises very clear (remind him that requests and promises are the language, the social currency, of business).
- Finally, do not shelter Scott from the consequences of his poor decisions about his relationships. Like money or an opportunity poorly spent, Scott may not miss the integrity of his relationships until it is gone.

Problem: *Sexual harassment.*

Situation: An employee has complained about the distinctly sexual nature of another employee's comments or actions. You don't want to lose either employee.

Suggestions: Discuss this complaint with the offending employee immediately; he or she is alleged to be inflicting abuse on a co-worker, and you and the company cannot and will not allow any harassing behavior. Sexual harassment is not the same as sexual discrimination, which directly or indirectly treats employees unfairly based on their gender. Sexual harassment is assault, and employers must regard it the same way as any other physical abuse. Once you are aware of it, you must take action. Seek the advice of your personnel manager immediately for your specific policy. The employee's complaint may become a lawsuit, so begin documenting every conversation, action, and agreement that demonstrates that you took the complaint seriously and made a genuine effort to rectify the situation. You can expect anyone accused of sexual harassment to deny any malicious intent, dismissing the charges as a misunderstanding. Perhaps this is a case of simple misunderstanding; you cannot be a judge or jury, but you can facilitate their discussions to reach a simple resolution. As their manager, you must alert both employees that accusations like these have destroyed careers and will not be taken lightly by the company. You must tell them both that you will not allow someone to be vilified by unsupported accusations, nor will you allow harassment to continue.

Problem: *An ongoing conflict between two employees who are each other's peer.*

Situation: Mary and Mark do not like each other and have demonstrated an inability to work together effectively. Left apart, they are fine workers, but the nature of their work requires them to occasionally join forces as a team. Are they allowed to continue to make life miserable for each other and the rest of the team, or does one or both of them have to leave?

Suggestions: You cannot control anyone's feelings or attitudes, but you have a lot to say about their performance. Make it clear to each of them that their poor attitudes are affecting their performance ratings and the productivity of the team; consequently, if they cannot work out their differences like mature adults, you will have to make the decisions for them. By explaining the larger picture, you are giving them the opportunity to resolve the problem on their own, which will, of course, result in a more permanent solution. At the same time, you are laying the necessary groundwork for termination of one or both should it become necessary.

Safety Problems

Problem: *Alcohol or drug abuse.*

Situation: No one can deny that this is a serious offense for the manager involved. About 10 percent of the population can be classified as problem drinkers or alcoholics, and some of these people may work for you. The number of people abusing other substances is also growing, although estimates vary widely from industry to industry. The chances are very good that you will have to deal with this issue at some point in your supervisory career.

Suggestions: Begin to document specific instances when you observed the employee on the job in an impaired condition. Consult with your personnel department or employee assistance counselor. Following are some of the major questions and considerations that will arise.

- Is performance negatively affected? If you cannot document poor or deteriorating performance, it will be very difficult to defend any disciplinary action you might take. As the abuse problem continues and/or increases, it will certainly affect general performance or cause lateness or absenteeism at some point. If these symptoms are present, they can become the basis for disciplinary action.

- Should you confront the employee directly about his or her abuse? Probably not. The employee is likely to deny the accusation and you may succeed only in cutting off communication. If the situation escalates to intervention by a third party (yes, the employee may sue you), your lack of experience in making clinical assessments will undercut your defense. Generally, it is best not to use words or phrases to the employee such as "drunk," "stoned," "on something," or "how many did you have?" Your discussion with the employee should be limited to what signs you see—deteriorating performance, patterns of lateness or absenteeism, and impaired physical condition, to name a few.

If an employee reports for work obviously under the influence of either alcohol or drugs, you should:

- Describe to the employee what you observe: slurred speech, incoherence, inappropriate responses, poor reflexes, red eyes, loud voice, inability to focus, silliness, or other unusual behavior.
- Tell the employee that it is your judgment that he or she is incapable of working safely and you, therefore, will not allow him or her to go to work.
- If you have access to a medical facility, insist the employee see a doctor or nurse. The employee can legitimately refuse, but if he or she does comply, then trained medical personnel can diagnose alcohol or drug abuse.
- Tell the employee that you will make alternate transportation arrangements. You or a co-worker, security personnel, family member, police officer, or cab driver can be enlisted to take the employee home. Do not let the employee drive himself home without making such an offer. If you do, your employer may be liable if there is an accident. Making such an offer is the right and safe action to take, and it strengthens your employer's defense if you are sued for liability. Later, tell the employee that you are concerned about the situation and strongly suggest he or she see a doctor or counselor.
- Involve the employee assistance counselor in this situation as soon as possible.

Problem: *Horseplay and other hazardous behavior.*
Situation: The possibility of injury to the employee or to co-workers makes horseplay or the like a serious violation of the rules. If, however, horseplay has been tolerated or condoned in the past, you will have difficulty upholding any disciplinary action.
Suggestions: Standardize and publicize safety rules that clearly prohibit unsafe activities. Explain the disciplinary consequences for violation of these rules, and then make your position credible by strict enforcement. Expect that

new rules will be tested until they are demonstrated to be supported by management. Safety rules should be practical, enforceable, and consistent.

On-the-Job Problems

Problem: *Poor retention of superior employees.*

Situation: Bernard, Hans, and Ruth are bright and capable workers who recently expressed a desire to move on to bigger and better assignments. Because the company was unable to offer them what they wanted, they all quit the company. How can a manager attract and hold good employees?

Suggestions: It's been said that good employees won't stay and poor employees won't leave. Retaining quality people long enough to recoup the company's investment in them will challenge you to challenge them. By enriching their jobs with lateral assignments, special projects, cross-training, and advanced training, you can keep them from outgrowing their jobs too soon. You can also help retention by keeping their advancement expectations realistic; do not promise them a rosy, but unlikely future because they will only become frustrated with you and the company sooner. Finally, look for other ways the company can meet their personal needs without promoting them or granting high pay increases, such as enhanced benefit packages, extra professional exposure or recognition, and personal relationships that inspire loyalty and commitment to the company's larger mission.

Problem: *Unacceptable quality or quantity of work.*

Situation: Shirley is a well-intentioned lab technician, but lacks some of the important skills required to do her job. Jeff, on the other hand, has the skills to do fine carpentry work, but has an attitude problem that slows him down and makes him careless.

Suggestions: Shirley has a "can't do" problem—she lacks skills that she can acquire through training. Jeff has a "won't do" problem—he has the skills and knowledge he needs and his performance has been acceptable in the past, but he apparently lacks motivation. In each type of case, you must: 1) communicate clear performance expectations, and 2) establish a performance pattern conflicting with those expectations. From this framework, you can direct and even insist on changes. Shirley must demonstrate proficiency; Jeff must exhibit new behaviors. Also, there must be consequences for poor performance: either proactive attempts to improve skills, for example, or reactive demotions, transfers, withholding of raises and promotions, or increased accountability ("I want to meet with you twice a week until this situation is corrected."). Termination is possible.

Problem: *Excessive absenteeism or tardiness.*

Situation: A five-man repair crew has developed some bad habits. As a group, they have a higher-than-normal absenteeism rate, and they have been observed reporting to work between 10 and 20 minutes late most mornings. Their previous supervisor did not make an issue of this because he wanted to be able to ask them to work extra time on a short notice. You initially believe they should show up on time and still work the extra time. After all, the schedule and type of work is clearly outlined in the job description; they knew what they were getting into when they took their jobs and they are well paid when they work the extra hours. What should be done, if anything, about the casual work schedule?

Suggestions: First, you must decide what is considered an acceptable degree of lateness. Many managers believe that clock-watching is an obstacle to getting results; others believe that if a person can be consistently late, he or she can also be consistently early and therefore can be expected to get to work on time and do their job without making a large issue about the time clock. Approaches to this will vary from organization to organization and frequently from work unit to work unit within any given organization. In any case, as with other performance concerns, a pattern of unacceptable action must be documented before any disciplinary action can be taken.

Problem: *Scheduling conflicts with shift workers.*

Situation: This problem competes with keeping the coffee pot filled for the problem most often discussed. How can you be fair to everyone unless you rotate, and how can you routinely and fairly decide a schedule that is constantly changing?

Suggestions: Don't make the problem worse than it needs to be. Hire people for specific shifts. Keep recruiting people until you find the quality people you need who prefer the less popular shifts. And don't treat them like second-class citizens, chronically short of support or direction. Rearrange your schedule so you can see them occasionally. Whether they're nurses or printers or drivers or overseas operators, they need to know they are an important part of the organization, too.

Problem: *Undeserved, but expected, pay increases.*

Situation: Tom may be a swell guy, but he's only a mediocre performer on a good day. Unfortunately, you have ducked the tough conversations about his disappointing performance too long, and now its time for his compensation review. Since you haven't said anything to the contrary, he believes he is doing a fine job and therefore entitled to a raise. How do you tell someone they will not get the raise they expect?

Suggestions: There is no painless way to make up in a hurry for missed opportunities to communicate about performance. Do not let this opportunity pass. If you don't utilize this opportunity to at least begin to discuss your concerns about his performance, you—and the good performers on your team—will continue to pay extra for mediocre performance. Give Tom less than he expects so that you get his attention; get past the "But I thought I was doing fine" part of the conversation as quickly as possible; and then help him focus on the areas of his performance that require improvement. He owes you a good day's work, and you owe him clear feedback on how he's doing and fair rewards for good performance.

Problem: *Falsifying records.*

Situation: Abigail, one of your equipment operators, is discovered to be fabricating output reports or quality control measures.

Suggestions: Falsifying records is grounds for termination or suspension, but you must be certain that she is guilty. If you allow her to remain, you are taking a risk with her future credibility (why wouldn't she do it again?), the integrity of your record keeping system (if she can get away with it, why can't others?), and the results of your department (quality or quantity of output may suffer because you obviously don't take the reports or measures seriously). Whether she stays or goes, you must document the incident and the substance of your discussion with her.

Problem: *Insubordination.*

Situation: Frank is your estimator, but he is not your friend. One day, without any obvious reason, he refuses to provide you with a quote. You say, "Excuse me? I mean I want you to do this now." He dismisses your request with a flip remark and saunters off. It is obvious to you that he is testing your authority. Good estimators are hard to find; should you just let this pass?

Suggestions: Insubordination is not insolence. True insubordination is the outright refusal to carry out a legitimate direct order. If the manager's request is within the subordinate's assigned duties and if it does not place the employee in a demeaning or unsafe position, the request is considered legitimate and must be carried out immediately. If the employee contends that your request is unsafe, you should refer to the safety manual. If that is unclear or if the employee still objects, immediately involve your safety officer or a higher level manager.

Problem: *Un-teamlike attitude among work group members.*

Situation: Personality conflicts are bogging down your work team. Everyone seems to be having a bad day, every day. Egos are commonly getting in the way of performance, and productivity is suffering.

Suggestions: It's time for some team-building exercises that cause your people to recognize and work for common group goals. Contact your personnel or training department representative for exercises that might work for your group, or consult the resources at your local library.

Problem: *Stealing.*

Situation: Eric has been caught in the act of pilfering company property. Naturally, he says this is the first time he has ever stolen and he'll never do it again. You want to punish him. What can you do?

Suggestions: As long as the incident is documented, this is justification for immediate discharge. You can recover some of the loss by using this incident to reevaluate your security procedures. Are your people naively allowing a "come and get it" attitude to prevail?

Problem: *Neglect or negligence.*

Situation: A press operator damages a switch that requires several days and thousands of dollars to repair. Meanwhile, the schedule is thrown into turmoil and several other workers stand idle. You are angry and frustrated. What should you take into consideration before summarily firing this operator?

Suggestions: Cool off, then trust your judgment. How strong a disciplinary action you can take depends on the direct and indirect costs caused by the employee's action and whether or not that action was willful. If this operator is normally a conscientious and valued employee, minimize the damage and try to keep everyone productive while the equipment is being repaired. If this is not the first time something like this has happened, you may be dealing with an inattentive, thoughtless, or even dangerous employee. If this employee is an accident waiting to happen, be grateful no one was injured or killed, document the incident, and terminate him or her.

Problem: *Abusive language.*

Situation: Ruth does not consider herself unusually sensitive or prudish, but she has finally complained to you about a co-worker who apparently uses inappropriate language routinely. Sometimes the language is just mild cursing, other times it is to or about co-workers or customers. How much can you expect to change this type of behavior? *Suggestions:* Discuss this problem immediately with the offending employee to get the other side of the story. Establish this as a performance problem by linking it to the negative reactions of co-workers and customers. Clarify your expectations; as with chronic lateness and excessive absenteeism, a pattern of unacceptable behavior must be established before any disciplinary action can be taken.

Chapter Fourteen

Assertiveness and the Virtue of Saying "No"

Assertiveness is an intensely personal communication skill that deserves some special attention by the new manager. Imagine how this recently promoted new manager feels: "I'm really frustrated because I can't say no to my employees or my boss. I'm too worried about losing their affection and loyalty. Then I feel worse because they probably lose respect for me when I don't stand up to them."

Many new managers are confounded with the trouble they encounter when talking to people. Somehow, they believe, all of the anxiety that accompanies difficult communication was supposed to disappear after they achieved the managerial ranks. "If I'm already in charge, why do I need to learn to be assertive?" they ask.

TO BE OR NOT TO BE: ASSERTIVENESS DEFINED

Assertiveness is a communication skill characterized by positive, direct, honest, and confident expressions about your ideas, feelings, beliefs, needs, or rights. It is an interactive communication skill that signals the following to those you work with:

"I don't and won't beat around the bush with you. I say what I mean and mean what I say."

"I'm striving to make my message clear and easy to understand. My messages aren't intended to manipulate; I won't play communication games that blame, confuse, or inject emotion into an otherwise rational discussion."

"I try to choose the right time to say what I have to say, taking into consideration your feelings and rights. For example, I'm not insensitive to the fact that you have your own problems that make it difficult to listen to me. I won't give up my right to my say, but I will be considerate and wait for a better time."

"I believe all of us share certain rights, no matter what our position in the organization":

> The right to express our thoughts and feelings, provided we do not violate the rights of anyone else.
>
> The right to be treated with respect.
>
> The right to defend ourselves.
>
> The right to say no without feeling guilty.
>
> The right to ask for what we want.
>
> The right to make mistakes as long as we take responsibility for our actions.
>
> The right to choose when to be assertive.

"I'm willing to listen to you when you assert your ideas, feelings, beliefs, needs, or rights. I'll listen to you when you are angry or critical without reacting in a similar fashion. I'll be glad to hear you give feedback as well as you take feedback."

Assertive behavior is an expression that attempts to assert your rights and enhance your message, but not at the expense of others' rights or feelings. It is a recognition that aggressive, confrontive, and passive behavior almost always confuse the message being expressed because they are dominated by emotion. It's hard to respond clearly and openly while under a verbal attack!

People are not born assertive. They learn to use the skills of assertiveness the same way they learn to sing, negotiate, and speak in public. Like all skills, your assertiveness will improve with practice.

WHY IS ASSERTIVENESS AN IMPORTANT SKILL TO LEARN?

Assertiveness is important because you're going to need it every day you are a manager. You are the target of everyone else's communication games, but you cannot allow yourself to play them in response. Your employees will try to manipulate, mislead, and misdirect you. They will lie to you, directly and by omission. They will direct their anger, frustration, anxiety, and guilt toward you, whether you deserve it or not. You will see them at their worst, so you must be at your best in order to express your message clearly, fairly, and exactly the way you mean it.

The payoffs for developing your assertiveness skills are as varied as your communication patterns. Just imagine how much easier your job will be when your employees, peers, and boss all understand you, and feel they have been treated fairly in the communication process. You are certainly unleashing much more of your personal power when you assert yourself, but at the same time, you are making it possible for others to do likewise by setting the standard and providing the example for clear communication.

Ultimately, the purpose of developing a repertoire of assertive communication skills is to increase your effectiveness in professional and social situations. This purpose is based on the assumption that people are more likely to achieve their goals by letting others know what they feel, think, and want.

ASSERTIVENESS APPLIED

So how does a person become assertive? It's simple: by becoming the most persistently fair and straightforward communicator he or she can be. This means to do the following:

- Describe directly and completely the situation or behavior of the people who you are dealing with.
- Describe your feelings.

- Explain how others' comments and behaviors have affected you.
- Focus your comments on results and observable behavior (which you can change), not personalities (which you cannot change).
- Empathize with the other person's position.
- State briefly, firmly, and specifically the alternatives or changes you would like to occur.
- Provide feedback.
- Invite feedback.
- Listen attentively and uncritically without beginning an internal discussion with yourself.
- Make sure you understand each other's interpretation of a problem before moving toward a solution.

It also means to *not* do the following:

- Misrepresent, withhold, or lie about information (your long-term integrity and credibility are at stake).
- Manipulate via emotions, exaggerations, melodrama, or compliments.
- Overload with too much criticism or praise at one time.
- Pass out unsolicited advice.
- Masquerade criticism or requests with compliments.
- Apologize unnecessarily or excessively.
- Send conflicting messages (your yes should mean yes, not yes, but . . .).
- Generalize.
- Evaluate the other's comments too quickly.
- React immediately to criticism (You should explore what is meant and ask for examples.).
- Jump to conclusions.
- Take over the decision-making process.

If you feel you would benefit from assertiveness training, check with your human resources department, trade association, or community college for possible classes.

Chapter Fifteen

Resolving Conflict

Surprise, surprise. No matter how hard you try, not everyone in your work unit is going to agree with each other. Conflicts are bound to arise because people have incompatible agendas—or at least that's their perception.

The principles of supervision we explored in Chapter 2 can be valuable guides to resolving conflicts that keep the organization from being effective.

Briefly, the process of conflict resolution can be described as a compromise between individual goals and organizational goals. The organization's goal is to function smoothly in the pursuit of its objectives; the goal of the individual employees is to have their personal needs for job satisfaction and financial security met, among others.

The principles of supervision are helpful because they organize the organization. This goes a long way towards minimizing the conflict that accompanies organizational confusion. By applying the principles of supervision, you can answer questions like, "Who's responsible for this?" and "Did you have the authority to make that decision?"

WHERE DOES CONFLICT COME FROM?

The organization versus the individual is only one of the potential conflicts in the workplace, of course. Others include co-worker versus co-worker ("I don't like you and I don't like working with you"), worker versus manager ("I disagree"), society versus the organization ("Stop polluting!"), and the government versus the organization ("Comply or pay the penalties"), just to name a few.

The same process of goal and attitude compromise works to resolve conflict between these groups. Two co-workers, for example, may disagree on how a certain job should be done. While one worker wants to do the job in the shortest time period possible, the other wants to do the highest quality job possible, regardless of the time it takes. Each is focused on the same task, but each sees the most important part of the task differently. To resolve the conflict and work together, each worker must be able to identify the other's goals and attitudes and reconcile them with his or her own.

THE POSITIVE EFFECTS OF CONFLICT AT WORK

Conflict is a natural element of any workplace. It is a by-product of the interaction between people with different ideas. As long as conflict can be resolved in a healthy, constructive, and orderly manner, short- and long-term benefits will result for those involved.

The following are some examples of how conflict and conflict resolution can be beneficial to both the individual and the organization:

New Ideas. Jim is anxious to prove himself in the engineering department and has argued persuasively to have new materials he learned about in school specified in a new product proposal. Dan, who has worked for the company longer, is threatened by Jim's ambition and has fought him hard on the material specification.

As the deadline for the proposal draws near, both Jim and Dan realize that they have to resolve their differences. While they both have good reasons for using their chosen materials, they both also have to admit that there are strong reasons to look for an alternative material.

After a frank discussion, they jointly commit themselves to finding the best material to specify by reviewing all of the important characteristics required for the product. The hardest task was ranking the importance of these characteristics in the order of importance to the project instead of by self-serving personal preference. They agreed to discuss each point until they reached consensus. They both realized that if their personal ideas could not stand up under tough scrutiny, the ideas had to be improved.

In the end, an entirely different material was found for the product specification. The new material was better than either of their personal favorites, and they admitted that they would not have considered the new material if they were not challenged to defend their first selections. An added bonus to the experience was a new respect for each other's professional abilities.

Quality control. The Miracle Drug Company was having a difficult time getting its new wonder drug approved by the FDA for distribution and sale because of prior quality control problems with earlier product launches by the company. Suspicious of yet another problem, the FDA officials were particularly wary.

The company management contended that all quality control problems stemmed from vague test and control regulations that often seemed contradictory. Both parties took great offense upon reading summary statements attributed to each other in a series of newspaper articles about the controversy. Trust and communication were breaking down, and the drug itself was receiving less and less attention. Finally, after many months without progress, the company replaced the product managers who shepherded the product through the approval process.

The new managers moved quickly to resolve the conflict between the company and the government. First, they examined the quality control procedures in the company's manufacturing process. The FDA's suspicions were at least partly justified. Changes were made to improve the weak links in the process. Then they scheduled an informal meeting with the regulators. They clearly outlined the company's goal: to gain approval for the manufacture and sale of the drug. They specified the requirements that they did not understand and requested clarification.

The FDA responded, but was still suspicious. Once the company's product managers were certain that they were in compliance, they requested another inspection by the FDA inspectors.

The inspection was the longest and most careful the company had ever undergone, but the FDA agreed that the company's procedures had passed with flying colors. The FDA explained that they had never really questioned the scientific basis for the drug; their reluctance to approve was rooted in their suspicion of the quality control procedures. The agency inspectors admitted that they did not make compliance easy, with regulations that could be misinterpreted or appeared to be in conflict with each other. They agreed to publish clarification for the benefit of other companies.

Improving productivity. Alan is struggling with an internal conflict that springs from his recent promotion to inspector of his company's medical product. Since Alan did much of the design work on the project, he feels particularly close to each phase of production and knows what to watch for.

It has become apparent, however, that he is not fast enough in his inspection. Alan's manager has indicated that if Alan does not or cannot complete his inspections faster, the problem is going to be taken out of his hands. "I trust you to be using your time conscientiously, but the bottleneck in your department is putting us way behind our deliveries," warns Alan's manager.

For his part, Alan is worried about missing a critical test and sending out a faulty product. He argues persuasively that he is the first inspector for this product, and since the product is used in hospital emergency rooms, the company's reputation and the lives of accident victims are at stake. Alan has begun to stay after work without pay to try to get caught up, which has led to numerous arguments with his wife and daily tension headaches. His anxiety has caused him to go even slower, and his productivity is deteriorating instead of improving.

Finally, Alan has had enough. He knows something has to give. Late one night, he faces the truth: He cares too much about "his" product and has too much of a personal emotional investment in it. He realizes that he must either wash his hands of it entirely, quit or get fired, or devise a better inspection procedure.

Within a few days, his productivity has improved dramatically. Without compromising the critical tests he must perform, he has identified many that can be handled elsewhere on the production line by the line supervisors. He has even eliminated some altogether. He begins to relax, and his personal productivity improves even more. Soon, he's ready to turn over his responsibilities and go on to his next assignment.

Improving workplace relationships. Fred and Abdul took an immediate dislike to each other. Each seemed to represent to the other much of what they each disliked about the world. Unfortunately, they both needed a job and ended up working across from each other in a small office.

Tension grew daily. Every motion, every comment became a bullet in an undeclared private war. Both began to show signs of fatigue, anxiety, and poor production.

Almost simultaneously, they heard each other reprimanded by their respective supervisors for disappointing performance. Sensing finally that they were seriously affecting each other in a negative way, Fred and Abdul began to change. They began to speak more freely, gradually learning to respect each other. Friendly competition replaced unfounded first impressions.

The conflict between Fred and Abdul forced them to change their behavior toward each other or suffer severe personal consequences. Their attitudes may not have changed, but their relationship with each other has been improved substantially because they each had a vested interest in resolving the conflict between them.

In each of these cases, there was a conflict between opposing factions in the workforce. In the course of the daily routine, these conflicts were resolved, leading to direct benefits for those involved. These cases are not unusual in any way; they illustrate that conflict and conflict resolution are normal in the workplace environment and exist at every level.

THE NEGATIVE EFFECTS OF CONFLICT AT WORK

Conflicts that cannot be resolved have varying negative effects in the workplace. When a conflict cannot be resolved or is resolved in a manner unacceptable to one or more of the opposing factions, a stressful situation develops that keeps the organization or the individual from functioning effectively.

One of the first negative effects of conflict manifests itself in a decline in productivity, which is often due to lost incentive or stress.

Another negative effect of conflict is one or more inappropriate behavioral responses to the conflict situations, which in turn leads to negative behavior that will probably cause more conflict. This could be expected, for example, if an employee submits a new idea to resolve a production problem and the supervisor flatly ignores the employee's input without discussing the merits of the idea. The employee naturally feels frustrated that his input is not appreciated or valued and may adopt an "I don't care" attitude, which in turn affects his performance. A more appropriate response would be to bring the idea up at a later time or regard it in a less personal way.

Following are some of the other negative behavioral responses to conflict situations:

Excessive absenteeism.

Unsociable behavior in the workplace.

Increased conflicts between co-workers, especially over seemingly petty matters.

Increased expressions of worker frustration, such as complaining about unsatisfactory conditions. Questioning of supervisor's authority, including direct insubordination.

Of course, conflict at work is only one possible reason for negative behavior. The manager is challenged to resolve conflict in an appropriate manner so that all parties can reap the positive benefits of the experience.

Since conflict is the natural, predictable result of the clash between goals and attitudes of the worker and the organization he or she works for, it is the manager's responsibility to control and resolve negative conflict as it occurs in the workplace and to prevent unnecessary conflict through appropriate planning. For example, when a company policy restricts the productivity of workers or when worker behavior affects normal operations, it is the manager who must take decisive action to correct the situation before it triggers conflict with other parts of the group.

Remember, not all conflict is bad. Some conflicts are definitely positive. The manager's goal is not to prevent or resolve all conflicts, but rather to prevent or resolve those negative conflicts that are unproductive, unnecessary, and not constructive.

The following are some guidelines for determining who or what is responsible for negative workplace conflict.

Workers are responsible for these conflicts:

1. Declining performance levels.
2. Unacceptable workplace behavior.
3. Inadequate skill levels to perform specified tasks.
4. Inappropriate interaction between co-workers.

The company is responsible for these conflicts:

1. Policies or procedures that lead to declining productivity.
2. Policies or procedures that lead to worker dissatisfaction.
3. Inadequate training programs for workers.
4. Policies or procedures that splinter the workforce.

Managers are responsible for these conflicts:

1. Unclear translation of corporate goals.
2. Inadequate or inconsistent supervision.
3. Inadequate or inconsistent coaching, counseling, and discipline.
4. Inadequate concern for worker needs and goals.

In many cases, there is a dual responsibility for conflict. If a worker's performance is declining, it may be the result of a poorly organized job definition or work station. Both the job definition and the employee's adaptation to the job must be clarified.

Once the conflict is identified, it is the manager's responsibility to take the necessary steps to reconcile the goal and attitude differences that will resolve the conflict. This is accomplished through confrontation, behavior modification, changes in organizational goals, or changes in the methods used to reach those goals.

Finally, since conflict by nature creates a certain amount of stress in all levels of the organization, it is the manager's responsibility to take some steps to help the individual or the organization cope with the stress.

Your personal leadership style, whether autocratic, participative, democratic, or laissez-faire (see page 93) will tend to dictate the nature and type of conflicts that occur, how conflicts are resolved, and the potential for new conflicts.

GUIDELINES FOR CONFLICT RESOLUTION

The first step to resolving any conflict is to identify and clearly describe the conflict. Unacceptable workplace behavior is symptomatic of a conflict. Declining performance, for example, or absenteeism or excessive arguing with other workers, are signs of conflict. In some cases, these are signs of a simple conflict which can be accepted at face value. In the case of absenteeism, the individual may have a chronic health problem that is beyond anyone's control.

However, it may also be a symptom of a larger, more subtle, and more complex conflict. The worker may be unhappy with the job or unable to get along with co-workers or managers or even have an alcohol or drug problem. All the manager knows is that he or she must take action to correct the inappropriate behavior. Good reason or bad, the worker is performing poorly.

Through an effective system of information gathering and performance measurement, a manager is able to identify and describe the true nature of the conflict. The information gathering process starts by noting and describing in specific detail the nature of the unacceptable behavior. If an employee is frequently late, mark it down: "Kathy was tardy on the 17th. 22 minutes late." You must document the negative behavior in detail with dates and descriptions of specific incidents.

You must also be prepared to explain how the negative behavior is affecting the employee's work performance. Is this behavior substantially different than that of other employees in the department? Have corrective measures been attempted before? Are any other symptoms apparent that might indicate other problems?

This first stage of observation prepares the manager to confront the employee and suggests possible corrective measures. By now, the manager should know what the surface problem is: a conflict between the individual and the company's policy on tardiness. He knows how extensive the problem is, including the specific dates of the offenses; he also knows how serious the problem is in comparison to other workers' behavior. Finally, he knows the nature of the short-term effects, including specific performance deficiencies. The questions that have yet to be answered are, Why is this behavior occurring? Is it a symptom of a larger conflict? These questions can be answered through a confrontation with the employee.

CONFRONTING THE PROBLEM EMPLOYEE

The manager must remember at this point that the goal is to solve a problem, not create another one with a destructive confrontation. Pick a meeting time that is as close as possible to the last offense, yet one with a minimum of anxiety for both of you. Be prepared, avoid generalities, and be constructive. Your task as manager is to correct or eliminate the problem or the problem employee.

A productive confrontation starts by presenting the problem from the manager's viewpoint. In the case of excessive tardiness, this means stating clearly that the employee is coming late to work on an unacceptably frequent basis and that this tardiness is affecting his performance and/or that it's contrary to company policy. The employee's response will be either an acceptance that the problem exists as stated by the manager or a denial of the manager's charges.

Through effective communication and the art of negotiation, managers can control confrontations with employees. This is important because the person who controls the confrontation tends to have the advantage in achieving the desired outcome. The person who is not in control can be led or directed by the other individual and usually has to accept some version of the other person's goals or needs.

The following are a set of rules or guidelines managers can follow to control a confrontation and keep it productive:

1. You must be able to state and identify clearly the nature of the conflict as he or she perceives it. The employee must know clearly the company's position in relation to his or her performance.

2. Be prepared to substantiate the stated position and anticipate the questions the employee might ask.

3. Listen carefully to the employee's response to the stated position. This response indicates the type of behavior the employee will use as a response to the confrontation.

4. Select a style of communicating with the employee that best counteracts any negative behavior by the employee. For example, if the employee denies the conflict or withdraws completely, try a more forceful approach.

5. Direct and redirect the conversation back to the nature of the conflict or the proposed resolution. This is accomplished by acknowledging statements that are not directly relevant (for example, "Yes, I understand that other employees have been late this week," or, "I agree with you that this is a companywide problem"), and then redirecting the conversation by restating the conflict at hand ("But I want to find a way for you to be here on time," or, "But let's talk about how the problem relates to your performance.").

6. Eliminate personal attacks and focus on problem solving. Employees tend to rationalize a situation or try to avoid it through personal attacks on the manager or other employees. Make it clear that personal attacks are not acceptable.

7. Learn to distinguish the reasons from the excuses. There are some legitimate reasons for unacceptable behavior or performance deficiencies, but excuses are just a way of avoiding problems.

It should be clear at this point that the key to effective communication in a confrontation situation is to focus on conflict identification and conflict resolution. Any communication that detracts from this goal dilutes the problem-solving process. Also, through careful listening and observation, the manager can identify clearly the employee's tactics and can determine the correct approach to counter unacceptable responses and maintain control of the situation.

NEGOTIATING RESOLUTION TO CONFLICT

In order to reach a conclusion that is acceptable to both individuals, a compromised or negotiated agreement must be reached. Effective negotiators can easily trade off points that are of secondary importance for a favorable agreement on the major points. The following guidelines will help you negotiate resolutions to conflicts:

1. Know what is your—or your company's—bottom line. The bottom line is the non-negotiable point or points beyond which you cannot compromise. Everything above the bottom line is negotiable.

2. Focus on negotiating the process or method that will be used to solve the problem rather than the problem itself. How an employee will get to work every day is open for negotiation. Whether the employee will show up or not is not negotiable.

3. Understand your position of strength or weakness. This involves determining whether the differences in the positions of authority change the bargaining position. Also, understand who will bear the negative consequences if a resolution is not found.

4. Give the employee an honorable method of retreat. People tend to respond irrationally when they feel backed into a corner with no honorable way of surrendering. By presenting options that accomplish the same thing, an individual feels that he or she has gotten out of the corner gracefully because he or she made some choices.

5. Recognize that the purpose of negotiating is not to be a winner or loser, but to reach a solution that resolves the conflict. In other words, accomplish the goal and don't worry about winning the battle of words. Making a concession so that the other person does not feel like a loser is acceptable, even preferable, if the main goal is reached. In addition, the chances that the final agreement will be carried out are better if the other person retains self-respect and feels that he or she has played an important part in reaching the solution.

Negotiation is essential for resolving complex problems and conflicts where it is important to have a consensus on several aspects of a conflict or when a trade-off of goals and needs is necessary. Effective negotiators have a clear understanding of what they want to accomplish, what they can afford to give up, and how the process of negotiation helps them achieve these goals. Effective communication and artful negotiation make the difference between stress-laden conflict situations and those dealt with smoothly and firmly.

In a confrontive situation, the employee's level of stress relates directly to his feelings about how he was treated, whether he had input into the process, whether he was listened to, and whether he feels good about the solution that was reached. You will be more successful in moving the discussion forward if you can keep everyone's level of stress down (including your own!).

In order to proceed, the employee must accept the manager's statement of the problem. The manager can draw upon his or her observation data to lead the employee to see the manager's point of view. If the employee continues to deny the problem as presented by the manager, either a conflict exists between the individual and the manager's authority (which may, in fact, be the real basis for the problem), or the observation by the manager was incorrect.

Once the employee and the manager have accepted a definition of the basic problem, a simple explanation by the employee will often identify and remedy the basic conflict. If the explanation does not address itself fully to the problem or the manager feels that there is something else at the bottom of this problem, further questioning can provide additional information. It is important for the manager to be able to interpret the employee's response and discern signs of underlying conflict. A few probing questions may be appropriate, but simply providing an atmosphere of trust and openness is usually successful. Given the opportunity, most people will talk about their problems.

After you have determined the type of conflict, you can set an attainable, measurable objective that will begin to remove, minimize, or correct the problem. The manager's role at this point is one of leadership. The manager is most effective when helping to answer the question, "Where do we go from here?" People caught in conflict have difficulty seeing and appreciating the problem-solving process from their limited perspective, and a third party can provide the critical guidance when they need it most.

Chapter Sixteen

Managing Stress

Soon after you take over as a manager, the stress of your new position may begin to catch up with you. Too many new tasks, too much responsibility, and too much to do in too little time may cause you to become tense and lose sleep at night.

You probably experienced the common symptoms of stress—physical tension, worry, frustration, boredom, or mental and physical exhaustion—in your previous job. None of these were serious problems as long as you dealt with them as they occurred.

But too much stress causes distress. While the normal stress of everyday life is generally healthy because it brings out the best in us, too much stress causes us to become dysfunctional.

Now that you have been on the job a few days, weeks, or months, how well have you adapted to the new, higher level of stress in your job? Are you continuing to deal with stressful situations as they come up? Certain work situations, habits, traits, values, and lifestyle choices tend to put more emotional and physical stress on an individual than others.

Use the following questionnaire to assess potential problems for you. If you answer yes to any of the questions, you may have identified a potential source of distress that requires attention now.

Stress at work

1. Do you perform any tasks that require strenuous physical labor?

2. Are there any potential health or safety hazards in your work?

3. Do you feel pressured to meet rigid deadlines?

4. Do you feel you have more work than you can handle?

5. Do you often feel bored at work?

6. Do you feel that your supervisors or your employees often don't understand you?

7. Do you feel that there is little possibility for advancement in your work?

8. Would you rather be someplace else besides work?

9. Do you feel that events in the workplace are often beyond your control?

10. Do you feel that you are not fairly compensated for the amount of work you do?

Stress at home

1. Would you rather be at work than at home?

2. Do you feel that your family doesn't understand your work? Do you think that they don't care about your work?

3. Do you feel that your financial situation is often out of control? Do you worry about money frequently?

4. Do you feel that your spouse often doesn't understand you?

5. Do you feel too tired to do anything when you get home?

6. Do you feel that you don't spend enough time at home? Does your spouse agree with you?

7. Do you often feel lonely at home?

8. Do you feel that events in your home life are often beyond your control?

9. Do you feel that your neighborhood is unsafe or dangerous?

10. Do you feel that it's difficult for you to relax when you are at home?

Stress caused by lifestyle choices

1. Do you smoke?

2. Do you drink too much?

3. Are you overweight?

4. Are you too important to your job to take a two- or three-week vacation once a year?

5. Do you feel that most events in your life are beyond your control?

6. Do you feel that it is too late in life to accomplish your goals?

7. Do you feel that the world is changing too quickly?

8. Do you feel that the world is a dangerous place in which to live?

9. Do you often feel depressed or sad for no apparent reason?

10. Do you look for things that can go wrong, rather than those that can go right?

11. Do you find yourself unable to keep the commitments you make?

12. Do you find yourself unable to maintain a long-term relationship?

You probably had to say yes to at least a few of the questions. When the symptoms of stress cause you to become less efficient, less effective, unhappy, or otherwise dysfunctional, your situation is becoming unhealthy. Pay attention to the source of stress. It may be time to employ new stress management techniques before your distress becomes chronic.

MANAGING YOUR STRESS

People who deal with stress successfully are those who take positive steps to deal with it. Following are some of the best strategies and techniques.

Regain a sense of control and competence. A person who feels that he or she has no control over the events of the day has little hope of taking action to correct them. This person will typically wait for someone or something to solve the problem, which of course never seems to happen. The more often this happens, the less confident a person becomes that he or she can ever resolve a distressful situation.

Practice taking action and solving problems in an area of your life where you do have control, even if it is unrelated to your source of distress. The success you experience in one area will help you in another. This will help break the cycle of poor confidence and poor results.

Learn to recognize the difference between the controllable and uncontrollable. Changing the company's profitability may be beyond your single-handed control. There can be no resolution, and therefore nothing to be gained, to be overly worried about it. On the other hand, your department's budget and your personal financial situation are well within your control.

Do not blame uncontrollable situations for consequences that could have been controlled. For example, just because the company is in financial trouble doesn't mean there is no hope for your individual financial security. In this case, it may be just an excuse to avoid responsibility.

Work toward permanent solutions. The best way to remedy the symptoms of stress is to stop the source of the stress. Consider changing your work habits or your lifestyle. Find new ways to accomplish your objectives. Clarify your priorities—if every problem is equally important, or if you focus on little problems as an easy way to avoid dealing with big problems, you are only making your problems seem larger by avoiding them.

Change what you can and accept the rest. Most problems are merely inconvenient. Most problems can be resolved, given enough time and your sincere commitment to keep trying to find a way to do it. Treating every problem as though your entire well-being depended upon the outcome fosters harmful emotional conflict. For example, failure to meet a deadline is not the end of the world. It may have serious consequences, but life will go on.

What can you do when you decide to meet head-on the problems causing you distress, but still find that appropriate solutions elude you? In this case, it is certainly acceptable to ask for help from peers or professional counselors. You may need to learn to live with the unresolved. Healthy people can put their problems into a realistic perspective and live satisfactorily with the consequences if the problem is not resolved favorably.

SHORT-TERM REMEDIES FOR THE SYMPTOMS OF STRESS

In order to focus on permanent solutions to the causes of chronic stress and distress, you will need to develop short-term strategies to cope with the symptoms of stress. The coping mechanisms and techniques explained below can be used to disguise or avoid stressful conflicts for awhile, but they are better used to provide the temporary relief you need to enable yourself to resolve conflicts.

Respect your limits. Everyone possesses a unique ability to handle stressful situations. Part of this ability is learned through work and life experience, but it is also related to natural, inborn traits. How much stress is healthy for you? Can you feel when you are out of your depth, beyond your healthy limits? Compelling yourself to become someone you are not is short-sighted in the extreme; do yourself, and your company, a favor and avoid those situations that might cause you to go beyond your acceptable limits.

Pace yourself. Avoid taking on more projects than you can comfortably handle. Do not get trapped by corporate cultures of "one-upmanship" and "superman/superwoman" expectations.

Improve your communication skills. Does crisis management make your stomach do flip-flops? You can eliminate a lot of problems before you get started by communicating effectively with your peers and employees. Try to:

- Give instructions specifically and clearly, and verify that you have been understood by asking the listeners to explain in their own words what you just said.
- Communicate consistently and predictably to gain the confidence of others.
- Take a break when confronted with an emotional situation; focus on constructive ways to obtain the results you want instead of your feelings or another person's attitude.

Learn to relax and sleep well. This is easy to say, but hard to do. Relaxation frees the body and the mind for a short time so they can recover and renew, thus preparing you for your next bout in the battle with stress.

The most common form of relaxation is sleep. When a person is asleep, the body slows down and is able to rebuild after the normal wear and tear of the day. The mind, while still active in dreams, is distracted from the troubles of the day. Dreams divert the conscious mind by employing the unconscious mind. When you awaken, your problem is still with you, but the short-term relief is helpful. A common behavioral response of a person under stress is to sleep more, to daydream more, and to fantasize more.

At times, the stress of conflict is so great that the mind cannot shut off and go to sleep. In this instance, a person has to find other ways to relax the body and mind. One method is to make a list of the concerns that are keeping you awake; for some people, the simple act of putting the concerns down on paper frees the conscious mind long enough to fall asleep. Alcohol or drugs are not good solutions because they interfere with the natural dreaming process that is so important to relaxation of the mind. If sleeplessness persists, professional advice should be sought.

Learn to relax during work. "Shutting off' during waking hours can be accomplished for short-term relief from stress with techniques that simulate the shift of your mental state from the conscious to the subconscious. Meditation, contemplation, and self-hypnosis are just a few of these techniques. In each of these techniques, through the process of suggestion, the body and the mind are disciplined to slow down on cue and diverted to spontaneous or dreamlike thoughts.

Do something completely different.   Other forms of relaxation that allow the body and the mind to get away from the problems of the day include sports and leisure activities, vacations, and other diversions. Since the mind cannot focus effectively on more than one thing at a time, activities that divert your attention have a relaxing and soothing effect.

Occasionally, it is important to get away completely from all the daily tasks and conflicts in the form of an extended vacation. People who take one or two days off here and there in lieu of an extended vacation do not allow themselves enough of a change to totally escape their problems. An annual vacation of at least a solid week is necessary for "decompressing" because people cannot just turn off their stress at will. Extremely active people in high-stress situations should try to take at least six weeks of vacation throughout the year.

For some people, the art of relaxation is not easily learned. They want to be on the go all the time, pushing and driving. Some people just can't sit still. Activity is good for these people, but the stress is not. In order to minimize the effects of stress, it is important to learn how to relax in a manner that works for you.

HOW TO HELP THE REST OF THE ORGANIZATION COPE WITH STRESS

An employer has a responsibility to help employees cope with stress that is resulting from factors in the workplace. More and more companies are taking the initiative to establish programs that teach health care, wellness, and coping techniques. Since companies already spend almost $17 billion a year on employee health care costs and related expenses, they also have a strong financial interest in the care of their employees.

The following are some of the steps an employer or manager can take to help the rest of the organization cope with stress.

1. Teach employees to be aware of stress. This means showing employees how to identify stress in various situations and how it affects their physical and mental well-being. (See the next section for some tips.)

2. Offer employees stress counseling. Teach employees how to cope with personal stress, resolve conflicts, and how to solve stress-related problems.

3. Make outside treatment services and other professional services available to employees.

4. Attempt to eliminate workplace factors that lead to stress.

5. Establish an open-door policy for talking about stress-related problems in the workplace.

EMPLOYEES CAN RELIEVE OR REDUCE THEIR OWN STRESS

Each employee has to learn to take personal responsibility for his or her own feelings of conflict and stress at work. This applies to you, too, so set a good example.

Many of a worker's problems with stress are self-inflicted. An employee must learn to avoid counterproductive pressure situations. This means not imposing unrealistic schedules or expectations upon himself or herself. For example, some employees feel compelled to meet the expectations of their managers, no matter how unreasonable and no matter the personal cost. They may be motivated by a desire to impress; they may be overcommitted because they do not know how to say no; or they don't know how to budget their time. Their efforts are laudable as long as they, and thereby the organization, don't suffer in the long run because of a stress problem.

When you see behavior like this in one of your workers, or when you see it in yourself, speak up and make some changes.

Another way to relieve stress is to finish some tasks, even if they are not the most important tasks. Juggling a dozen or so partly finished projects is wearisome because each has its own deadline and the effect of not resolving any of them is cumulative. Sometimes, you just have to stop, pick one of those projects you're juggling, and finish it. Not only does this remove the source of some of your stress, but the good feeling that comes with accomplishing something is a great tonic.

Try to resolve all conflicts as soon as possible after they come up. Write the letter, confront the performance problem, call the vendor, place the order, make the decision—whatever you need to do to short-circuit the buildup of stress. This "no baggage" approach may even earn you a reputation as a quick decision maker!

Finally, employees should be encouraged to take appropriate steps to stay healthy through intelligent personal habits, including proper diet, exercise, and relaxation. Don't be shy— if you really care about your workers, and if you see behaviors or lifestyle choices that may turn toxic for them, speak up in a friendly way.

HOW DO YOU KNOW WHEN YOU HAVE TOO MUCH STRESS?

Often, a person who is overcome by stress is too involved with the problem to recognize that the stress symptoms have become a major problem in themselves. Alcoholics are an excellent example. People who have tried to deal with stress through excessive drinking have a difficult time realizing that they now have an alcohol problem larger than the problem with which they started.

How much is too much stress? Since stress cannot be measured, behavior is the best guide. When a person has become dysfunctional at work, he or she has passed beyond the threshold of his or her capacity and needs to seek professional help.

Many behaviorial clues indicate dysfunction due to stress: inability to concentrate, forgetfulness, irritability, failure to keep old routines, denial of problems, excesses of all kinds, inability to remember or follow through with commitments, and so on. These are all minor dysfunctions warning of an impending system failure if constructive steps are not taken.

You can learn to be aware of your stress limits and remain sensitive to the limits of others. If stressful behavior persists for any length of time, do whatever it takes to "stop the dance" of the self-defeating behaviors.

BEYOND THE BREAKING POINT
AND THE TREATMENT OF DISTRESS

The human body and the human mind cannot tolerate an unlimited amount of stress. The limits are different for each person, and they may vary with the time and source of the stress. Once an individual has reached and gone beyond the breaking point, physical or psychological reactions occur that prevent the individual from functioning normally in the workplace and resolving even the most routine problems. In severe cases, a total breakdown occurs and the individual is unable to function at all.

At this point, there is very little a manager can do except identify the individual who has a debilitating stress problem and refer the person to an appropriate treatment program. The treatment of distress—the emotional and physical suffering resulting from too much stress—can and should be provided only by a professional trained in the treatment of stress and distress disorders.

Likewise, identifying an employee with a debilitating physical response to stress is usually out of the hands of the manager. Severe responses such as heart attack and stroke usually are an emergency situation referred to a physician immediately.

Your role is that of an early warning system for stress in the workplace. Because you know your workers, you are more likely than anyone else to spot the changes in behavior that signal a potential problem. When an employee is suffering from extreme physical exhaustion, insomnia, or other of the stress-related ailments mentioned earlier, no one symptom or event will give you the clue you need to understand his or her mental or emotional state. The small changes you see may signal a serious problem in the making.

Still, even though you are friends with this employee and know him or her quite well, the trouble signs may be difficult to observe. In fact, he is likely to try to mask his symptoms. For obvious reasons, you are the last person he wants to tell about his problems with stress.

You are doing an employee no favors by buying into his or her self-deception. Denial and efforts to maintain the illusion that "everything is just fine" or "everything will be just fine once this or that crisis passes" are dangerous. Since denial of the problem is a common response during distress, the individual may not think it is important to seek outside help. These people will show a high rate of absenteeism and their performance will have increasingly sharp peaks and valleys that reflect how well they are wrestling with their problems.

Being able to diagnose an employee with a stress-related emotional problem or a psychological problem is extremely difficult and is not for the untrained. The symptoms of one type of disorder can be very similar to another type of disorder and, in the case of alcoholism, the signs can be very well concealed. A combination of disorders may be present. The employee's work performance and/or his behavioral response to supervisory direction and relationships with other co-workers are the manager's only clues that there is a problem.

In many instances with psychological disorders, it is not the abnormal behavior which is the tip-off but rather the degree or severity of the abnormal behavior that determines whether the individual needs outside help to become functional again. The following is a list of signs to look for that may indicate an employee is near or beyond his or her breaking point.

1. Absenteeism (unexplained absences more than two or three different times during a month and excessive tardiness).
2. Sharp peaks and valleys in performance levels.
3. Sudden withdrawal from work situations and other workers.
4. Hostility or violence with other workers.
5. A lack of mental alertness.
6. Erratic or antisocial behavior.

To understand better how employees respond to distress, what the symptoms of distress are, and what causes employees to become dysfunctional in the workplace, it will be helpful to explore further the nature of physical and psychological stress disorders.

PHYSICAL STRESS DISORDERS

The human body is normally in a state of homeostasis. This means that the pulse rate is normal, as are the temperature, blood pressure, and respiratory rate. When the body experiences stress, the individual responds with the primordial "fight or flight" response. The fight or flight response prepares the body for conflict by increasing the amount of adrenaline in the body, increasing the pulse rate, blood pressure, and respiratory rate, and increasing the level of blood clotting agents. Digestive processes slow down to a virtual standstill. This response helps the individual deal with dangerous situations: He is better able to fight for his life or run for his life.

The mind does not cause the body to respond differently to a situation of actual physical danger and a psychological event. This means that when a conflict causes stress, it causes the same fight or flight reaction as the body prepares itself to meet the conflict. Unfortunately, this response causes a large energy loss and wears on the body's systems.

In most cases, through proper diet and rest, the body can restore itself quickly and function normally again. But when the body is not allowed to repair itself or the stress is continuous over a long period of time, the body starts to break down, resulting in physical ailments and a decline in resistance to disease and infections. In some cases, the breakdown is so complete that the body just stops functioning, such as in the case of a heart attack or stroke. The only real treatment of stress-induced physical disorders is rest and relaxation.

PSYCHOLOGICAL STRESS DISORDERS

Psychological stress disorders occur when a person is overcome by stress and the mental processes are no longer able to resolve the offending conflict. When psychological disorders go beyond the point where the manager can intervene with effective coaching and counseling or his problem-solving skills, professional treatment is required.

A psychological disorder will manifest itself in several ways, and it is important to be able to identify these and how they affect workplace behavior. The following are some of the psychological disorders caused by stress and how to recognize them.

Severe depression. The individual becomes extremely sad or melancholic and feels that there is no solution to the conflicts in his or her life. He or she feels a total loss of control and a sense of hopelessness. This is reflected in a withdrawal from work and life situations. The person is constantly tired and seems exhausted, yet sleeps more than usual.

Neurotic behavior. A person exhibiting extreme neurotic behavior is often termed a "bundle of nerves." This individual worries about everything and feels that everything is either caused by or affects him or her. This person is extremely sensitive to events and the attempts of others to help. Neurotic behavior is characterized by one or more of the following reactions: anxiety, compulsions and obsessions, phobias, depression, disassociations, and conversion of emotional conflict into physical problems.

Psychotic behavior. A person with a psychosis has a major mental disorder whereby the personality is disorganized and contact with reality is usually impaired. A functional psychosis is usually manifested in schizophrenic or manic-depressive behavior. This person's behavior is erratic and will appear irrational; it may include violent episodes.

Burnout. When an individual burns out, he or she has become saturated with stress and his or her system no longer responds. This person will seem to be numb to surrounding events and unable to react constructively.

Other psychological disorders relate to the fact that the mind has a difficult time distinguishing the difference between real and imagined situations. When stress it too great for the conscious mind to handle, the subconscious mind takes over and tries to substitute more pleasant imaginary situation. This explains, in part, why some people under stress seem to be out of touch with reality.

Diagnosing a psychological disorder is extremely difficult and complex, even for the experts. The criteria are basically subjective and the diagnoses of one professional and another can differ. The manager will never be in a position to recommend treatment for a specific psychological disorder; however, he or she can help by being a good observer of changes in the worker and serving as an early warning system for stress-related trouble. The manager may be able to recommend a professional evaluation or opinion after the employee has exhibited a dysfunctional behavior.

Psychological disorders can also be addressed by trying to deal with the conflicts that caused the stress. This can be done either through counseling or by changing the individual's workplace stresses.

ALCOHOL AND DRUG ABUSE

In some cases, alcohol and drug abuse can be classified as a stress-related illness. The intoxicating effect of alcohol and drugs offers the individual short-term relief from stress by disrupting the normal thinking process and thereby diverting the individual's attention away from the stress. However, with the continual use of alcohol or drugs to relieve stress, the negative side effects become as serious as the stress and the original conflict.

The manager does not need to have a complete understanding of the underlying causes of alcoholism and drug addiction. What is important is that the manager recognize that the employee is not coping with stress in an acceptable manner and that the side effects negatively influence the individual's performance and the workplace as a whole. All a manager can be expected to do is to identify the individual with an alcohol or drug-related problem, confront the employee, and try to persuade him or her to seek professional evaluation and treatment. If there is no improvement, the manager may have to terminate the employee.

Chapter Seventeen

Developing Your Career

What's next for you? Are you taking care of your own career development as well as you take care of your employees?

We began this book by acknowledging that you must be doing a lot of things right in order to make the change from worker to manager. Now is not the time to slow down. Now you have some of the time and resources you need to make some significant investments in your own development.

We also asserted that most of what you're going to learn about your job is going to be learned on the job, while you are doing the work of managing. You learn on the job by observing, discussing, and finally doing the work. This is going to continue, so don't become fearful of making a mistake or two.

Your best route to personal development is to do your job as a manager exceptionally well. Remember the Performance Improvement Model? It applies here, too. Prepare to be judged on your performance as a manager. The good news is that no matter what happens to your industry or your company, your time as a manager will not have been wasted. Your skills and your accomplishments are portable.

HOW WELL ARE YOU MANAGING YOUR PERSONAL CAREER?

The five keys to successful personal career planning are the same as planning for your department: specificity, feasibility, a control system that updates the plan, writing the plan down, and periodic reviews of the plan.

The following questions will help you assess your personal career plans; note if they do or don't support your plans for your department or division.

1. Do you believe you can influence the future through your planning efforts, or is success a matter of luck?

2. Do you understand the similarities between planning for the business and planning your career? How is it different?

3. Explain how you go about "inventing" the successes in your career. Are you a successful planner?

4. Have you had to adapt your career plans recently to accommodate new information or a new situation? Do you still have confidence in your planning process? What have you learned from this experience and has it caused you to change your personal planning process?

5. What is your personal mission statement?

6. What are your three to five goals for the next three to five years?

7. What do you want to happen during the next 12 months? (Formulate your tactical plan.)

8. What are your top three priorities?

9. What are the dangers of spending too much time planning? (Clue: Rather than compressing all your planning activities into a single marathon session, it is

better to spread them out over several days or weeks so you have time to let ideas develop—and limit the plan to just two pages!)

10. How do you know when you are not following your plan?

11. When will you next review your career and life plan?

STAYING PROMOTABLE: HOW YOU CAN BETTER MANAGE YOUR PERSONAL CAREER

What are your personal long-term goals? Do they coincide with the company's goals? If your goal is to move beyond this managerial job, you'll have to demonstrate that you are ready for more of the same kind of responsibilities. Here is a quick recap of the suggestions we've made in this book that build and develop your career:

Refresh and reset your goals. Get some help to do this, either from your manager, mentor, or a colleague. Advice and feedback from someone older who has had experience with your company would be particularly helpful in pointing out opportunities and possible career paths. They also may be able to share insights about the company's long-term growth strategy, which will give you important clues as to how you should prepare yourself. Advice from a more experienced person will also help you keep your goals realistic: "Sorry, Janet, it is unlikely you can become a plant manager in less than five years," "Don't bank on taking over the new SuperDuper product line—I've seen that thing on-again, off-again a dozen times."

Get results. This is your job; this is why you are paid more than others. Of course, how you get results is usually as important as the outcomes, so short-term results at the expense of permanent progress is a poor bargain.

Continue to take care of the present, and the future will take care of itself. Keep your priorities clearly in mind: Now is not the time to forget to take care of your boss's needs, the mission of your department, or the details of your operation. The question you asked at the beginning of this book was, "Can I succeed as a manager?" Well, so far, so good, right? Now you should ask yourself, "Can I manage my success?"

Find ways to practice and develop your planning, decision-making, and communication skills. While many other types of skills are also important, these will remain the most important three far into your future. They will help you in more ways, more often, as your career progresses.

Practice managing changes. You are more than an administrator—you are a masterful change agent, leading the organization towards its prosperous future. If you can become good at this, you will be a valued contributor no matter how your job changes. Keep the following tips in mind when you cause change to occur:

1. Share your excitement about the upcoming change; people need this to replace their former vision.

2. Share as much information as you can about the change; this will help some people deal with their anxiety about the uncertainty while slowing the spread of misunderstandings and rumors.

3. Change means choices have to be made; let others participate in those choices so they have some ownership in the outcome.

4. Keep surprises to a minimum; communicating the plan in small, easy-to-understand steps reduces confusion and anxiety.

5. Go fast enough to keep people interested and motivated, but not so fast that uncertainty about the consequences becomes the dominant feeling.

6. Communicate your expectations for performance clearly and consistently.

7. Adopt a "can do" style for yourself, and reward others who do the same.

8. Highlight the benefits of the change as soon as they become real; let others know as soon as you can that the change is worth their extra effort.

9. If someone "loses" because of this change, be honest with them up front so they can prepare and change themselves into winners, too.

10. Change only that which is necessary to change; some familiarity with past routines and habits makes it possible to adopt new routines and habits.

11. Begin planning for the next change immediately; by the time you're ready for it, you will need it, because yesterday's "new" has become today's "old."

12. Finally, overcommunicate. Never presume that you have been completely understood, particularly by those who resist change for reasons of their own.

Plan, plan, plan—and then ACT. The planning skills you are developing for your job as manager are portable to your personal development, too. Following is a quick review of effective steps you can take to enhance your ability to develop and execute good plans.

1. Obtain your job description from your manager or the human resources department; clarify any inconsistencies or points of confusion with your boss now, while there is still time to make adjustments and while you are still getting used to your new roles. Plan to perform splendidly on every item for which you are accountable. As one managerial virtuoso put it: "If it's on the page, it better be on the stage."

2. Ask your boss again what his or her expectations are. Which projects or programs is he or she watching closely? Have they changed since you became a manager? Of course, as you make your own plans, you will want to pay special attention to these.

3. Talk to your employees and ask the following kinds of questions: What plans are under way for which projects? What problems with scheduling, budgeting, or delivery do you foresee, and what are your recommendations to solve the problems? Their answers will help alert you to plans made or not made by your predecessor and prevent surprises.

4. Obtain the formal and informal, written and unwritten, short-, mid-, and long-range plans that involve your department. Do you understand the organization's objectives and priorities? You need information now, so keep asking the people who can give it to you.

5. Begin making short-term plans for yourself immediately, and stick to them. Plan your day, your week, and your month as if your job depends on your ability to plan and follow through.

6. Finally, make sure that you keep the work moving and keep those around you well informed about what you are doing. If you discover that you cannot accomplish something for which someone else did the planning, communicate your scheduling problems immediately. Do not let yourself be victimized by someone else's plan; seize control as soon as you can, make the plans your plans, and begin building your reputation as a planner who can be relied upon.

Recruit a development partner.   Your development will be richer if you can give and receive support from a like-minded person in your company, or in a company like yours, who is experiencing similar challenges and satisfactions.

Cultivate your personal network.   These friends and acquaintances may last a lifetime, providing you with priceless insights, foresights, job leads, and customer and supplier introductions.

Seek feedback about your performance.   You cannot get too much, too often. Make sure that your perception of your contribution is shared by those important to your success.

Manage your manager. Learn what is important to him or her, then make that important to you. Does she value reports and plans? Master the word processor and give her the best reading she's ever had. Does he always put customer service above all else? Make the customers your passion. Innovation? Frequent discussions? Group meetings? Sales promotion? It doesn't matter—every boss is entitled to his or her individual style and approach. Your job is to take care of your boss, and that means supporting your manager's agenda. If you take care of your boss, he or she will take care of you. Knowing your boss well can save you enormous amounts of time, time that you can reinvest in your own agenda. A final word about your managing your manager: Never, never let your boss be surprised with bad news that you could have delivered first.

Manage your time. It's the end of the day. You've taken one too many phone calls and sat through one too many meetings. You're tired and frustrated. Where did the day go? Why can't you get done what you planned to do? Time management has suddenly become an essential skill. Your problem lies partially in the nature of your position. You're on the spot for everyone, so you're their target, friend, source of information and permission—it's no wonder you occasionally feel beleaguered.

Your problem may also stem from less-than-perfect control of your time. DANGER: This can kill your career, one minute at a time. Many books and courses about time management are available. The best of them talk about getting the best return for spending your time resources, not just how to be more efficient. The key to time management is effectiveness: It is far better that you do the right things inefficiently than do the wrong things efficiently.

The following suggestions will help you get started.

1. Practice managing short amounts of time, then expand your control as you get better at it. You're probably already doing this when you have an important and well-defined project. Take confidence in the fact that you have done this before on a small scale. You *can* do this.

2. Spend your best time on the important stuff (e.g., early morning hours, before everyone else's problems divert you).

3. Beware of the time wasters. They live where you work. Sometimes they look like friends and employees; sometimes they are old habits and comfortable routines.

4. Make the hard decisions early, as soon as you can. Delay can paralyze you because it becomes its own reward.

5. Do whatever it takes to solve the tough problems. Fretting about too many problems slows everything down.

6. Delegate. Managers get results by working through others.

7. Stick to your plan. It's a good one—certainly better than no plan. The largest benefit of your plan is to remind you what is most important to do, so your time is always well directed toward the work that matters most.

Finally, have fun. If you don't enjoy managing, don't do it. If you do enjoy it, I wish you a full and happy career; may you always make your numbers.

Good luck! You have a great start to your managerial career!

Index